Hubert E.H. Jerningham

Norham Castle

Hubert E.H. Jerningham
Norham Castle
ISBN/EAN: 9783744795364
Printed in Europe, USA, Canada, Australia, Japan
Cover: Foto ©ninafisch / pixelio.de

More available books at **www.hansebooks.com**

Norham Castle

BY

HUBERT E. H. JERNINGHAM, M.P.,

AUTHOR OF "LIFE IN A FRENCH CHATEAU;" "TO AND FROM CONSTANTINOPLE;"
AND TRANSLATOR OF THE LIVES OF "SIXTUS V.," BY BARON HUBNER;
AND "LORD BYRON," BY COUNTESS GUICCIOLI.

EDINBURGH:
WILLIAM PATERSON
MDCCCLXXXIII.

PREFACE.

THE present work has no further aim than to provide for the inhabitants in the neighbourhood of the Tweed as it rushes to its mouth, and to those whom its natural beauties and its legends and historical traditions attract to its banks in the summer months, a portable compendium in a readable form, as I trust,—
" Oh that I had the art of easy writing,
What should be easy reading...."
—of the vast amount of information contained in those volumes of which I have given a list, and from which I have mostly worked out this history.

The exhaustive works of Dr Raine and Mr Hutchinson are neither portable nor within the means of the greater number of those who would like to know more about this corner of England; but it must be allowed that they are so complete and so admirable in themselves that they deserve to become more popular, and I trust that some enterprising publisher will give them some day the honour of a cheap edition.

I have embodied in this history all the information

supplied by the documents which Dr Raine has published in his History of North Durham, and which relates specially to the old Castle of Norham; but my constant desire has been to connect with the general history of England the several events to which these documents refer, and I must own that, with this particular object in view, I have had very great difficulty in keeping to the subject, and not wandering from it into a History of North-East Northumberland, taking up Mr Hodgson's interesting volumes from Morpeth, where he leaves off.

Though the task is, I feel, but very imperfectly accomplished, still I venture to hope that the stirring events connected with Norham, and which constitute the pride of this fortress above all other Border castles, have been brought forward more strongly than they have yet been, and that my volume on this ground will find favour on the Borders.

Few places indeed can boast of more interest, whether to Englishmen or to Scotchmen, in the advantages which incidentally, of course, Norham was the means of procuring to either country.

Thus the introduction of Christianity into the north of England, and its first footing in Norhamshire by the successful missionary work of Scotch monks; the disputes before Norham which eventually gave Scotland a Bruce; and the poaching affray at Norham which brought about the union of the two countries through the marriage of James IV. and Margaret Tudor, are so many facts which point to the most stirring events in the history of both countries.

Then the gradual establishment of the natural boundaries of England and Scotland, and the necessity for their protection arising out of the predatory and martial spirit of an age not shaped into permanent form, together with notices of those men who have played a conspicuous part in the history of Norham, and in particular of those families who have carried their honoured names down to the present day, whether on the Border or in the adjacent counties, such have appeared to me natural chapters of a popular history; if I have bestowed upon their rendering some labour and much sympathy, I have taken especial care not to prejudice the work by inaccuracies, so far, at least, as lay in my power.

Though a book for leisure hours, I have not allowed it to lose its strictly historical character, which will account for the many quotations and translations which I have introduced within the text; indeed, wherever it was possible, I have given the words reported to have been used, whether rightly or wrongly, so as not to lose the force of the old English or Scotch manner of expression.

The only attempt at general history of the county is made in the third chapter, when I conceived it necessary for the general reader to gather from its perusal how invariably Scotch and English made Northumberland the battle ground on which they fought out their grievances and revenged their losses.

These few remarks may perhaps not indispose the reader to forgive the absence of strictly fresh material in consideration of the manner in which the old has been patched up into a new form, a form which, I trust, may enable others, if not myself, to discover more documents relating to Norham than the scanty bills of cost of repair and reports on its state of decay which have yet come to light, and for which, however, the historian can never be grateful enough to Dr Raine.

But some day we may see documents of greater value issuing from the record chests of old Border families,* and until then I can only offer this contri-

---

* If these pages stimulate such a research I shall not consider this volume as having been written without profit to the cause of historical inquiry, which, by the way, owes so much in the present day to the excellent family biographies lately issued in Scotland.

bution to Border literature with all heart and all humility, and say with Lord Houghton—

> "These harmonies that all can share,
> When chronicled by one,
> Enclose us like the living air,
> Unending, unbegun."

HUBERT E. H. JERNINGHAM.

LONGRIDGE TOWERS,
BERWICK-ON-TWEED, *February* 1883.

CONTENTS.

CHAPTER I.
INTRODUCTION OF CHRISTIANITY IN NORHAMSHIRE   PAGE 1

CHAPTER II.
DESTRUCTION AND RECONSTRUCTION   18

CHAPTER III.
SETTLEMENT OF GEOGRAPHICAL LIMITS   36

CHAPTER IV.
FLAMBARD   60

CHAPTER V.
PUDSEY   80

CHAPTER VI.
KING JOHN   103

CHAPTER VII.
EDWARD I.   123

CHAPTER VIII.
WALLACE AND BRUCE 142

CHAPTER IX.
EDWARD III. 167

CHAPTER X.
MARRIAGE OF JAMES IV. . . . 185

CHAPTER XI.
FLODDEN 209

CHAPTER XII.
PATCHING UP . . . 235

CHAPTER XIII.
DECAY 261

APPENDIX 279

NORHAM CASTLE.

CHAPTER I.

INTRODUCTION OF CHRISTIANITY IN NORHAMSHIRE.

A.D. 635.

> " Time's an hand's breath : 'tis a tale,
> 'Tis a vessel under sail ;
> 'Tis an eagle in its way,
> Darting down upon its prey ;
> 'Tis an arrow in its flight,
> Mocking the pursuing sight."
> —*Francis Quarles*, 1634.

NINE miles south of the wonderful isle of Staffa, with its overhanging pillars and wave-worn Gothic arches, stands the little island of Iona, better known in days of yore as Hy, Y, or Iona.

On a fine day in the early months of the year 563, a little vessel with its sails full set to a westerly breeze might have been seen making its way through the Sound, and coasting the rocky shore, which glittered like marble in the rays of the sun, casting at last its anchor in a small creek which now bears the name of Port na Churaich, discharging there its monkish freight—thirteen holy men from Ireland, one of whom, "a man of angelic features," they saluted as their Father, their Abbot.

This was the great St Columba, who, fired by the love of that faith which filled his life and fed his every want, had come to preach the gospel of Christ to the Pagan Picts, and convert them to Christianity.

Conall, then lord of the western Scots, had promised him a peaceful landing in the island of Hy, and a further grant of land for the erection of a monastery.

The first days of the stay of these pioneers of Christianity were busy worldly days, for on the island there were no huts to protect them, and the produce of the soil, which was little cultivated, owing to a more than scanty population (there were only five families on the island), barely sufficed to meet their own limited requirements. But as the French poet Racine has so beautifully put it—

> Aux petits des oiseaux Dieu donne la pâture
> Et sa bonté s'étend sur toute la nature.

In the service of God Columba and his followers could never want, but they had a great mission before them, and it was necessary to build a home which would to them be the dear Alma Mater from which they would go forth with courage, and to which they might return with confidence or for spiritual comfort.

So monks and all set to work to build a monastery

such as they had already helped to rear in Ireland, and it was not long before an eminence having been selected, it was surrounded by a "vallum" or fosse, and a cell for the Abbot and founder was built with joists upon the eminence.

After this mark of respect to the chief of the little band, other cells were built for the brethren of wood or wattles, and then successively the church, *oratorium*, peeped its head above the huts, and the refectory, the MS. room or library, and the offices were raised.

When these were finished the monastery proper was complete ; but hospitality being the prime virtue of all conventual establishments in former days, more cells had to be constructed for the reception of strangers ; and as the fields to the west began to yield the crops due to the agricultural labours of the monks, and the cattle which grazed on other fields to the east were ripening for slaughter, outer houses were constructed, such as the *Bocetum*, cow byre, the *Horreum*, granary, the mill, with a pond and a mill stream, the stables, *prædium*, and the harbour, *Portus*, for craft of various sizes.

When all these were completed, that monastery was erected which was to be the parent stem from which in a near future the glorious abbeys of Melrose and Lindisfarne were to spring.

Like a fortified village at first, the fame of Iona

soon spread, and the monastery developed into a town. The descriptions of it which have reached us, together with the accounts of the life led by these early monks of the pre-Benedictine order, remind us both of the still existing picturesque and interesting Greek monasteries in the Levant, and of the ascetic rules instituted by St Basil which the Greek monks are supposed to follow.

The monasteries of Athos in particular remind one of what we learn was the primitive manner of building in England fifteen hundred years ago, but while the rule throughout the east was to stamp out all remains of Pagan times by building churches on the sites whereon had stood their temples, and using therefor the stones and marble with which most of them had been so beautifully reared, in the British Isles a stone building was unknown, and only wooden edifices could be constructed.

To protect property therefore, natural defences, such as ravines and water, were made available at first, and later a wall encircling the *hamlet* or agglomeration of huts was added to the strength of the place, but it was only a little before the Conquest that stone buildings became the fashion.

These old monasteries had no architecture, but within the space contained by the ditch, *fosse*, numberless courts and huts were erected, just as are now seen in the monasteries of the East.

Windows were mere apertures, as huts only existed for night protection and the silence of prayer. The hut reserved for the sanctuary was only a little taller than the rest, and was surmounted by a cross, while the abbot or prior's hut was on an eminence to indicate command.

The same rule exists among the monks of Athos, where chapels all stand apart from the main buildings, and the œgoumenos has the loftiest apartment when he does not occupy a dependency of the building.

The analogy between these pre-English monastic institutions and those of the East with which they were contemporary is curious to note.

One day as St Columba, from his favourite seat outside the abbot's cell, was watching the waves in the near distance as they rolled tempestuously against the rocky shore, moved by a wind of no common violence, he suddenly called to his followers, and said, "Brethren this is Tuesday, to-morrow is a day of fasting, but as a guest will arrive, the fasting will in his honour be dispensed with."

On the morrow, as the storm of the preceding day had developed in intensity, and the waters in the Sound had become a sea wherein it seemed as if nothing could live, St Columba ordered a repast to be prepared, and water to be ready to wash the feet of the coming guest.

The tempest which raged at the time was so great that even his followers, who never doubted their abbot's word, gently remonstrated as to the possibility of any stranger crossing the one mile strait in such a storm; but before evening a little boat was seen approaching, and labouring through the trough of the sea. Presently it neared the Iona shore, sometimes lifted up on the crests of mountainous waves ready to dash the small craft against the rocks ahead, and at others swallowed up, as it were, within the grasp of giant waters: it came nearer, however, every moment, and at last the creek was gained.

A rush was made to the harbour to greet the stranger, whose coming had been prophesied, and whose advent must be of good augury, since even fasting was to be dispensed with in his honour.

The welcomed stranger was a young man of comely face and gentle manner, between eighteen and twenty-two in age. His bright blue eyes spoke as to his gentleness, while his tall and graceful figure bore visible testimony to the nobility of his birth.

Making his way to the little cell on the eminence, outside of which sat the giant-sized Columba, he knelt before him, asked for his blessing, and the favour of being admitted among his disciples.

Aidan, or Aedhan, was his name, and in him Columba saluted the first apostle of Northumbria, the future founder of Melrose and of Lindisfarne.

He had come to Iona to learn the ways of piety and devotion under St Columba, and for forty years he remained a monk of his order, leading a life of penance, privation, and prayer, well befitting the training necessary for his coming apostolate.

In 597 St Columba died, having succeeded in making Christians (at least in name) of the Picts whom he had come to Iona to convert, and was succeeded at first by Conin, one of his original twelve* disciples, and next by Fergna, who in 616 received as a guest a little boy of great promise, intelligence, and natural courage, who was only twelve years of age, and who was sent by Donald the Fourth, King of the Picts, himself a late recruit among the Christian ranks, to be baptized and instructed in the religion of Christ.

The boy was called Oswald. He was the second

* The number 12, as typical of the twelve apostles, was a favourite number during the early ages of Christianity, and was introduced in almost every department of monastic economy.

An abbot generally had twelve disciples. Twelve years were the usual term of ecclesiastic penance and monastic reclusion.

In the same way the sign of the cross was employed as a "signum salutare" on every possible occasion, and the saying went that "Hy was remarkable for its 360 crosses."

These usages are in the present day as much in vogue in the Greek Church as they were in the earlier days of the Christian Church in England.

Mystic numbers and mystic signs have always had mystic influences, and hence great vogue; it is only the sense of veneration and respect that defines their character and limits their usage.

son of Ethelfrith, King of Bernicia and Deira, who was slain by Redwald, King of the East Angles, on the banks of the Idle, in Nottinghamshire, and with his mother Acca and his brothers had fled for protection to the court of Donald, the Pict, across the Firth of Forth.

Abbot Fergna placed him for instruction under the special charge of the gentle Aidan, and thus began at an early age that friendship which seventeen years later was to bear such fruits, and make of Northumberland the stronghold of Christianity in Great Britain.

The child took a great fancy to his master, and was never rebuked by Aidan when he told him of his boyish dreams, how he intended to recover the throne of his father either for himself or for his family by the strength of his arm, or when he gave vent to the aspirations of a naturally ardent nature; but Aidan worked unceasingly to inspire the boy with that faith "which knows no obstacle," and to create a soldier of the cross, while educating him in those virtues which would make him a military commander.

Nor were these efforts lost, for years later, in 633, when Oswald, by the death of his elder brother, slain by the hand of Ceadwalla, Prince of Cumberland, had become heir to the thrones of Bernicia and Deira,*

* Bernicia was properly the country which extends from the

and was hastening to avenge the death of Edwine, he found at once the occasion to display his military qualities and his Christian faith.

Coming upon the army of Ceadwalla, on the banks of the Tyne, in the neighbourhood of Hexham, and noticing the number of the enemy, he reflected that with his own few followers, stout as they were, he had but small chance of success: then suddenly the lessons of Aidan came back to his mind; the vision of Constantine before the battle of the Milvian bridge and the motto beneath the golden cross on the azure sky, "in hoc signo vinces," recurred to his memory, and forthwith planting a wooden cross in front of his camp, he called to his men to kneel.

"Beseech the living and true God," said he, "of His mercy to defend us."

He then displayed his little army in battle array,

Tweed to the Forth, and included Edinburgh (Edwin's city), while Deira comprised the actual Northumberland. From Deira came the fair-haired boys who, in the slave market in Rome, first attracted the notice of Pope Gregory the Great.

"From what country do they come?"

"They are Angles."

"Not Angles, but angels."

"From what province?"

"From Deira" (de irâ).

"From the wrath of God called to Christ's mercy. And what is the name of their king?"

"Alla."

"Who shall sing alleluiah."

and awaited on carefully chosen ground the attack of his foe. But the steadiness of purpose of the Christian commander, helped by the strength of a faith which had then to give the first proof of its staunchness, coupled with the knowledge of their fate if defeated, gave to these stout Northumbrians, at whose limited ranks the Pagan prince is known to have laughed, the strength of a powerful army; and before the day had run its course, Ceadwalla had followed Edwin to the grave, and in the language of those days the conquerors "*could scarcely believe their eyes on beholding the slaughter they had made*" of the enemy they had dreaded so much before the battle began.*

* "It was necessary for the assailant to be extremely cautious, and on that account he drew up his forces in a position of great natural strength some seven or eight miles to the north of Hexham. Here there is a plateau of very considerable altitude, which, without any artificial appliances, presents the appearance and the advantages of a vast fortified camp. The ground on the summit is tolerably even, and must in Oswald's time have been covered entirely with heather.

"The place, which in honour of the vanquisher in the fight, has for many centuries been called St Oswald's, bore, previous to the struggle, the name of Heavenfield, an allusion, no doubt, to its lofty and exposed position. Oswald could not have drawn up his forces in a better place. Along the whole of the western side the platform was unassailable, for it is protected by the steep rocky banks which descend abruptly to the river of North Tyne, and overlooks Walwich Grange and Chesters, with its Roman bridge and camp. Towards the south also, and on a portion of the eastern side, there are hills and fells of no mean altitude. Across the upper end of this great natural fortification ran the

No wonder that Oswald's standard became then the symbol of that faith which, like unto Constantine, his prototype, had given him such an unhoped

Roman wall, but between it and the northern side of the plateau there is a space left on which a small army might be drawn up to a most advantageous position for repelling any attack. A scanty force in the rear would be able to guard the western, southern, and eastern sides so well that no assailing body could carry these heights; and if it could, the Roman wall, a stout barrier, in many places at least six feet in height, would still protect the greater part of Oswald's troops.

"Oswald, therefore, never fearing any onset from the rear, took up a position at the north-west corner of the plateau, behind the wall. In that angle, protected in one way by the wall and in another by natural rocks, there is a clear space of nearly a hundred yards, and there probably on the mound which the chapel now occupies, Oswald set up the famous wooden cross to be the standard of his men. With rocks in front and the wall behind, it would be difficult to capture it; and its defenders, who cannot have been very numerous, would be conscious of their security. We may be sure also that Ceadwalla would make his great effort at this point, for the loss of the standard was considered equivalent to the ruin of the army. To the north-west there is a long stretch of pasture land, and the eye passes on to Swinburn and Humshaugh, and far up the river in the direction of the Cambrian Hills.

"Over this ground it is probable that Ceadwalla brought his men, and the opposing armies could see each other for miles before they closed. The troops of Ceadwalla would break like a wave against the rock-bound corner in which the cross was standing, to be cast back again with little or no difficulty by its defenders. The assailants, foiled as they must have been at this point, would naturally move towards the east, where the ground is less steep and more open, and in that direction the battle seems to have been decided. The success of Oswald and his men would inspire them so much that when the enemy tried to attack them on more for victory. It is not a little curious to note that the arms of the see of Durham are even now a cross *or* between three lions rampant *argent* on a field *azure*.

The three lions *argent* were a subsequent addition to the original standard, a cross *or* on a field *azure ;* in other words, the golden cross in the sky of Con-

even terms, it could have no chance; the assailants if they got so far, would be pushed back, and the fight deserting the corner in which the cross was standing, would go roaring eastwards. 'There is a fame,' as Leland tells us, 'that Oswald won the batelle at Halydene, a two myles est from St Oswalde's axche!'

"There is a place called Hallington in the direction mentioned, and it was here probably that the battle was fully won. Ceadwalla would be thus cut off from his retreat, and the defeated chieftain crossed somehow or other the Roman wall, and hastened towards the south across the wild moor with the pursuers after him. Over the heather he would go, down the green banks below it, through the Tyne, and at a distance of eight or nine miles from the battle-field he was caught and killed at a little beck called Denises burn, a tributary of the Rowley-water. He would be entangled in the network of woods and streams when he was slain.

"The battle-field was, of course, the object of great veneration, for a great Christian victory was won there. This was the first occasion on which the sacred symbol had been erected in this part of the country, and the cross that Oswald set up stood in its place for many years, working miracles, as we are told, and attracting the steps of many a faithful pilgrim. In after times the monks of Hexham paid it a yearly visit on the fifth of August, the day on which Oswald himself met his death in battle, and with solemn rites and ceremonies chanted a service for his soul. A church was soon reared by them, and still there is a chapel to mark the spot which they honoured."—Preface to the "Annals of Hexham," by Dr James Raine, Surtees collection, vol. xliv., page xi.

stantine which Oswald gave to Lindisfarne, the original see of that of Durham.

In the enthusiasm which followed his success, Oswald sent a messenger to his protector Donald, and requested, while informing him of his victory, that he would communicate with the Abbot of Iona, so as to send him missionaries who could help him in the work of converting his kingdom.

The request was not long in being conveyed, nor long in being obeyed. Cornan was chosen for the apostolic work; but we know from tradition that his temper and manner were not suited to the rough and ready Northumbrians of those days, and after toiling heavily, laboriously, and zealously for a few months, he wisely resolved on returning to Iona.

One quiet and lovely afternoon he reached the little harbour from whence he had departed with so much hope and expectation only a short time back, and now with tears in his eyes he knelt before his abbot, declaring that a mission in Bernicia was contrary to the will of God, for they were people too stubborn and barbarous for His grace to make way into their hearts.

Presently Aidan gently remarked that perhaps Cornan's own stubbornness and severity were at fault, and that, no doubt forgetting the precepts of the Lord, he had omitted to give them like children the milk of gentle precepts, before treating them like men to the meat of harsh and ponderous dogmatism which they could not understand.*

These words had a remarkable effect, for it being resolved in all minds present that failure was not a word which a community of holy men could admit in the service of God, it occurred equally to every one that he who could speak so well and point to the cause of Cornan's failure with such an unerring finger, was the only person fit to remedy the past, and plant firmly into the Pagan soil of northern England the standard of the cross.

Once the choice had fallen upon him, Aidan made hasty preparations for departure, and we may gather from the principal features of his character which have been handed down to the admiration of posterity, that his requirements were as few as his ardour and zeal in the service of the Christian faith were great.

Bede says that "it was the highest commendation of his doctrine with all men, that he taught no otherwise than he and his followers had lived: for he

* According to Bede : " You did not at first, conformably to the apostolic rule, give them the milk of more easy doctrine, till being by degrees nourished with the word of God, they should be capable of greater perfection;" and according to Franciscus Godwin, Cornan's return is thus explained :—" Quod arcana Dei sublimia magno verbum strepitu, ad ostentationem potius iugenii quam auditorium rudium utilitatem ingereret, ut nec bonos mores concionibus suis induceret, nec ad suspicienda fidei initia animos blandioribus præceptis molliret."—Dempster's "Hist. Eccl.," vol. i. p. 124.

neither sought nor loved anything of this world, but delighted in distributing immediately among the poor whatsoever was given him by the kings or rich men of the world."

As soon as the boat which conveyed him from the island to the mainland had landed him and his followers, he pursued his way through town and country on foot, inviting both rich and poor wheresoever he saw them to embrace the mystery of the faith, or strengthening in that faith those who had already embraced it, and stirring one and all by words and by action to the practice of alms and good works.

In this wise—for he ever refused to ride—he reached the kingdom of Bernicia, and perceiving near the sea shore, not far from the mouth of the river Tweed along which he had walked for some days, and which had become as a friend to him, an island standing somewhat in a similar position to that of his beloved isle of Hy, which he had only left at the call of duty, he fixed in his mind that there henceforth his residence should be; then making his way further to Bamborough, which was already asserting its title to a royal town and castle, he presented himself before his friend and present sovereign, King Oswald, who welcomed him with all the warmth of early friendship, and offered him any place he might choose in his dominions for a permanent establishment.

Aidan asked to be allowed to found his monastery and establish his see on the island which he had perceived on his way to Bamborough, and which was visible from that royal residence.

Thus it was that the island he chose was the island of Lindisfarne, and before the end of the year 635 he had established himself in a temporary home, and had begun his missionary progress which was more helped by his example than his eloquence, for he could not speak the English dialect, and the king himself interpreted* for him to the thousands who were attracted by the kindly manner of the charitable prelate.

It is interesting to know from the MS. of Symeon of Durham, that the boundary of the diocese of Lindisfarne granted to St Cuthbert, its abbot, fifty years later extended on the east from the Tweed to Darmouth, then along the course of the Darn to Hebburn Bell, a hill in the parish of Chillingham, and hence along the Till, which is called Bremish in its upper waters, to the Tweed, wherein it flows at Tillmouth, in the parish of Norham.†

Though these limits, together with the country that lies between the Edre, viz., the Blackadder and

---

* " Contigit ut evangelizante Aidano, qui Anglicum perfecte non noverat, ipse rex suis ducibus et ministris interpres existeret."— Dempster's " Hist. Eccl.," p. 153. Bannatyne Publication.

† " Symeon Dunelm," p. 140.

Whitadder, which flow into the Tweed close to Berwick, and the Leder, viz., the Leader, which flows into the Tweed below Melrose, were confirmed to St Cuthbert by Egfrid, one of the successors of Oswald, it is more than probable that they were for the most part the original limits of the diocese established in favour of St Aidan by Oswald; and this is the more likely that further south, where the Cheviot range begins, was the limit (near Yetholm) of the missionary progress of Paulinus, the disciple of St Augustine. It is also certain that in conferring a see upon his friend, Oswald consulted his wishes, and the above limits, embracing as they do most of the country which he had traversed on foot, had naturally occurred to him as those which he would himself prefer.

It was only later that the diocese was extended; but the fact remains, that, while Bernicia and Northern Northumberland were the last portions of the British Isles to receive the teaching of Christianity, it was from Norhamshire and the Isles, in other words, from the County Palatinate of the See of Durham, that the light first dawned upon the banks of Tweed, a light destined to shine with a purity and lustre with which no other part of the kingdom can vie.

For did not Lindisfarne become the Holy Island, and did it not, besides its founder, furnish apostles to all England and martyrs to the faith, and above all, shine as the abode of St Cuthbert, the glory of Northumberland ?*

Thus, indeed, the spot which was to become a military stronghold in future time against the Scots, and with which we are particularly concerned, was first seized upon by a Scottish monk to form part of the basis of his Christian invasion of Northern England.

* "Northumbria had done its work. By its missionaries and by its sword it had won England from heathendom to the Christian Church. It had given her a new poetic literature. Its monasteries were already the seat of whatever intellectual life the country possessed. Above all it had been the first to gather together into a loose political unity the various tribes of the English people, and by standing at their head for nearly a century to accustom them to a national life, out of which England as we have it now was to spring."—Green's " History of the English People," p. 34.

CHAPTER II.

DESTRUCTION AND RECONSTRUCTION.

A.D. 867.

> "Nor did St Cuthbert's daughters fail
> To vie with these in holy tale:
> His body's resting-place, of old
> How oft their patron changed, they told;
> How when the rude Dane burned their pile,
> The monks fled forth from Holy Isle."— *W. Scott.*

FOR two centuries Norham, or Ubbanford,* as it is called in some of the older MSS., was but a prettily-

---

* I take this to be a mistake, and that it should have been Ufan-ford—the high ford, or ford above; and as the word "above" in the Scandinavian languages is pronounced "oben," "oven" the transition from the Saxon *f* to the Danish *v* and thence to the German *b* is not difficult of explanation, considering the Scandinavian races which for three centuries overran the north of England.

In Bosworth's Anglo-Saxon dictionary, published in 1838, and which is a most elaborate and interesting work, it is remarkable that not a single Saxon word is given beginning by *ub*, which would naturally lead one to suppose that Ubbanford, as given by Hoveden, was written as he pronounced it himself. On the other hand the words *ufan, ufa, ufane, ufon,* meant above, high, upwards, as *ufan and neodane,* above and beneath.

The matter is of no great importance, except that it has not yet been commented on as far as I know.

situated and well-wooded village on the banks of the silver Tweed.*

No church had arisen before the time of which we are writing (830) to mark the place as a dependency of the great monastery in its neighbourhood, but a convenient fording-place across the great river had already imbued it with life, and attracted under the shelter of the overhanging rock, † which protects its entrance, many a friar in his lonely communings with nature, as he bent his way from Lindisfarne into Northern Bernicia, or returned from his missionary

* "The greater part of English soil was still uncultivated: a good third of the land was probably covered with wood, thicket, or shrub, another third consisted of heaths and moor. In both the east and the west there were vast tracts of marsh land: fens nearly one hundred miles long severed East Anglia from the midland counties: sites like that of Glastonbury or Athelney were almost inaccessible. The bustard roamed over the downs, the beaver still haunted Beverley, huntsmen roused the bear in its forest lair, the London craftsmen chased the wild boar and the wild ox in the woods of Hampstead, while the wolves prowled round the homesteads of the north."—Green's "History of the English People," p. 62.

"In the British, Roman, and Saxon times, Northumberland abounded with forests and groves of oak and other timber . . . Cheviot is upon record for its oaks and brushwood in such abundance that it was called the great wood of Cheviot by way of eminence."—"Natural History of Northumberland," by John Wallis, vol. i. p. 135.

† Beneath it was a well still called the Monk's Well, the pure and crystal waters of which not only refreshed the weary pilgrim, but had the power, so the legend said, of bestowing on barren wives the blessings of maternity.

wanderings to his beloved home in the Farne Islands.

We can imagine little oratories erected here and there in the woods, where pilgrims knelt to ask the protection of God through the intercession of St Cuthbert; or little crosses studded about to remind these still early Saxon Christians of St Oswald, who fought beneath its shade, and still more that they must combat the difficulties of life with the blessing of Him who died upon the Cross.

Apart from these tokens of a living faith, no stone structure had raised its head in St Aidan's immediate district—the Norhamshire of the present day. But between the years 830 and 845 there was a great commotion in the pretty village. Bishop Egfrid * had given orders for the construction of a stone church in honour of St Peter, St Cuthbert, and St Ceolwulf, and it was whispered everywhere that the body of the latter was to be translated to the new church, an honour which was greatly enhanced by the fact that not only had Ceolwulf been a bishop of Lindisfarne, but he had also reigned as king over Northumbria in its more glorious days.†

* The last bishop but one of Lindisfarne.
† "Not long after King Egfrid had given Melrose and Carham to St Cuthbert, and the lands belonging to these monasteries, he was succeeded by Ceolwulf, son of Cadwinning (730), who, giving up his crown and his wife for the love of God, came to Lindisfarne with much treasure, caused his beard to be cut, received the

Great activity prevailed, and by a singular concurrence of circumstances the church was finished as Lindisfarne was being destroyed, and its monks from the distant Kyloe Hills could, over the plains before them, behold its blazing pile. It was finished as the supremacy of the Northumbrians over the Saxon Heptarchy was passing away; it was finished as the old distinctions between Bernicia and Deira were disappearing in the conquest of the Scots over the Picts, and as the great river which flowed beneath its shade was asserting for the first time its natural right to be recognised as a frontier between England and Scotland.

St Aidan's remains were back in Iona; St Oswald's and St Cuthbert's relics were fugitives from the land they had blessed; Lindisfarne was a ruin, its monks put to flight; Norham alone, as a bright diamond escaped from the old diadem, remained to prove to future ages that within its district Providence chose the spot from which to diffuse Christianity over the north of England.

tonsure, and gave to St Cuthbert the property called Werchewurde (Warkworth) 'with its appendages.'

"Postea dedit Egfridus rex Sancto Cuthberto Mailros et Carrum et quidquod ad eam pertinet. Non mullum post hunc Egfridum successit in regnum Ceolfus filius Cadwinning, seque Sancto Cuthberto subdidit, et dimisso regno cum uxore pro amore Dei se cum magno thesauro ad Lindisfarnense monasterium contulit, barbam deposuit, coronam accepit et Sancto Cuthberto villam dedit nomine Werchewurde cum suis appenditis."—"Symeon of Durham," xxxviii.

Already in 787 the Danes, with three ships, had made a descent in the south, and had slain Byrhtric, King of the West Saxons, who had hurried from Dorchester to meet them as "strangers or traders, and not as plunderers."

Six years later, in 793, Northumberland was startled by "excessive whirlwinds and lightnings, and fiery dragons flying in the air," omens which were looked upon with horror as presaging further calamities, and shortly after, "on the 6th of the Ides of January (viz., the 13th of January 794), the heathens lamentably destroyed God's church of Lindisfarne, trampling on the sanctuary with polluted feet, casting down the altars, carrying off the treasures of the holy church, slaughtering and drowning many of the brothers."

In 795 they made a descent upon the monastery of Jarrow-on-Tyne, but failing in this object of destruction, they sailed away. A storm, however, overtook them, and they were wrecked near the monastery of Wearmouth, in sight of Jarrow.

Forty years after this, in 833, the Danes rebegan their incursions to the south of the Tyne, but in 866 they landed in East Anglia in great force, and under the command of Ingwar and Ubba, sons of Rednar, Lodbrog, who had been cast a year or two before into a dungeon filled with venomous snakes by Ella, King of Northumberland, they overran Northumberland in their desire to avenge Rednar's death.

Indeed, if the Northumbrians dreaded the Danes and their cruelty, the cruel manner they revenged themselves on Ella showed that there was ample justification for such dread.

"They tore his ribs asunder, they folded them backwards till he presented the appearance of a spread eagle, and then the raw and reeking flesh was sprinkled over with salt to increase the intensity of the inflammation."

Such was the lot of the last Northumbrian monarch. After him, under Egbert, who was only their lieutenant, the Danes allowed the country north of Tyne to become the prey of marauders and pirates, "not caring to give them any protection," and returned to York to establish themselves firmly in East Anglia.

It was then that the pillaged church of Lindisfarne, from which, during the forty years' truce from their invasion, Bishop Egfrid had caused the royal remains of St Ceolwulf, the king-monk, to be translated to Norham, was totally ruined. It had almost risen again from its fallen state, and was peopled once more with a numerous colony of monks. Presently the news arrived that Halfdene, a Danish pirate, was marching north from Tynemouth Priory, which he had left a mass of smoking ruins, and, "burning all he found in his way, tearing the babes from their mothers' breasts, spearing man, woman, and child whom he encountered," was bent upon the ruin of Lindisfarne.

St Cuthbert had left a legacy in the shape of a hope that his bones should never be allowed to be touched by unchristian hands; and so great was the veneration for his memory, so powerful the influence of his name over the simple monks, that even in that hour of danger, with the full knowledge of what atrocities had been perpetrated on former occasions, and of the cruel fate which awaited them should the Danes reach their monastery before they had found refuge in flight, their first and only care was how to save the body of St Cuthbert,* and preserve it from insult.

The wish of their patron and saint had been prophetically expressed in 687, and now in 867, by a curious analogy of figures, the wish was to be carried out.

Bishop Earldulf thereupon summoned into his presence Eadred, a man of known piety, who was abbot of the monastery at Carlisle, and it was decided to open the coffin of the saint, wherein they deposited the head of King Oswald, some bones of Bishop Aidan, and other relics; then closing it reverentially, they bade adieu, with tears in their eyes, to the monastery they all loved so dearly, and set off on that wonder-

* He died 20th March 687, at the age of fifty-three.

ful pilgrimage which was to last so long, and be fruitful of so many romantic incidents.

Coming to the sea-shore with their treasure, the monks found it was spring-tide, and that they would have to wait; but suddenly "the waters formed a wall on their right hand and on their left hand, and a dry road and a clear path was before them on the sands. When all the men, women, boys and girls, herds and flocks, sheep and cattle, had entered on their path through the sea, the waters, following their steps directly behind them, returned in a wonderful manner to their former level."

The mainland reached, the seven laymen who carried the body and all the followers made their way to the Kyloe Hills, from whence they saw the burning of the monastery they had left behind them, and where they received the intelligence which made them resolve on proceeding further.

"For the space of seven years," writes Reginald of Durham, "St Cuthbert was carried to and fro on the shoulders of pious men, through trackless and waterless places: when no house afforded him a hospitable roof, he remained under the covering of tents."

From Kyloe they made for the Tweed across the forest, and at Norham they took a boat and towed the body up the river to Tillmouth, thence to Carham, and thence to Melrose; but as the old monastery of Melrose had been destroyed by the Scots, they had to retrace their steps, and the next place we hear of their being at is Ellesden, the modern Elsdon, not far from Morpeth, in the Redesdale Hills. "From Elsdon," says Archbishop Eyre in his life of St Cuthbert, "they probably followed the course of the Reed, passing what is now Bellingham, where the Reed falls into the North Tyne; then they would follow the North Tyne, and then the South Tyne to Haydon Bridge, six miles west of Hexham, and thence to Bellingham," where they learnt that Hexham was a mass of ruins.

The untiring band then set forth for Cumberland, where tradition reports they rested at Carlisle, Salkeld, Edenhall, Embleton, and Lorton, near Cockermouth.

Westmoreland was next visited, and "Dufton Fells, three miles north of Appleby, afforded them a very secure shelter," but they had at length to leave it, and tarried at Clifton, near Penrith, before they entered Lancashire.

Here they halted for a while at Hawkshead, where the hills between Windermere and Coniston provided the most perfect security; then at Kirkby Ireleth; Aldingham, east of Furness, Over Kellet, north-east, of Lancaster; Lytham, near Kirkham; Mellor, three miles from Blackburn; and Halsall, some ten miles north-west of Ormskirk.

Yorkshire was the next stage of their pilgrimage; an undefined pilgrimage, it is true, for it was a procession of men searching for some resting-place for a body which they carried with them, and which had been dead nearly two hundred years.

Burnsal, in the West Riding, saw them arrive. Ackworth, near Pontefract; Fishlake, near Doncaster; and Peasholme, a suburb of York, were their next stages, when they made their way to the Tees, following its course to Forcett, near Richmond, in the North Riding.

Traces of their journey through Barton, near Darlington; South Conton, near Catterick; and Marsk, among the Swaledale hills, then back again to the neighbourhood of York, at Overton, are extant, as well as at Kildale, near Stokesley; Kirk Leatham, south of Redcar; Wilton; Ormsby and Marshton, near Stokesley.

Finally they got to Durham county, and rested first at Darlington, Billingham, Redmarshall, Chester-le-Street, and Durham.

I have followed in this nomenclature the names given in Archbishop Eyre's book, carefully compiled from the existing republished MSS. of Reginald of Durham, which forms the first volume of the valuable series of the Surtees publications, but I have endeavoured to give as rational an itinerary as the anarchy of the times and the fear of the monks combined make it possible and likely for them to have followed.

In Simeon of Durham and in Reginald of Durham, reference is made to Ireland and to Scotland. With regard to the former country, Mr Surtees supposes that they went direct to the west coast. This may be possible, as they went to those countries where they could easily have got a ship to take them across, but it was not their intention on leaving Lindisfarne.

It has struck me that their object was especially to find a safe resting-place as soon as possible, and that Melrose in Bernicia was their first goal, and the Tweed the natural road to it. Mailros was the child of Lindisfarne, and St Cuthbert had originally come from Mailros.

But the ravages of Kenneth the Scot, the victor of the Picts, had laid Mailros in ashes, and made all the country east of Strathclyde Scottish territory. An allusion, therefore, to Melrose in Scotland is not only interesting, as historically correct at that early period, but reconcilable with the itinerary given.

Melrose given up, Hexham Priory was another natural goal; so was Carlisle, so was Penrith, so was York, so was Chester-le-Street.

Here they arrived in 883, when King Alfred had restored peace to the Christians in the north, and Halfdene was dead; and here the See of Lindisfarne was continued for 113 years, while the body of St Cuthbert was placed in the sanctuary of the church. Earldulf, who had fled from Lindisfarne, was the first bishop of Chester-le-Street; but the Danes had not finished their work, and still the body of St Cuthbert had to be "protected from heathen hands."

In 995 "an oracle from heaven instructed Bishop Aldhune to fly with the incorrupt body." He started with it and all his people for Ripon, and in 999 it was deposited at Dunholme, "where a little church of wands and branches was built wherein the body was laid, till a more sumptuous church was built wherein he might be enshrined."

This was Durham Cathedral, and St Cuthbert at last found a resting-place within the apse and behind the altar-screen or reredos which crossed the church at the apse.

No dead body, however, ever gave more trouble. In 1277 his tomb within the new feretory was spendidly improved; but in 1537 Dr Ley, appointed by Henry VIII., with Dr Henley and Mr Blythman, to suppress monasteries, had the tomb opened, deprived it of its jewels, "found the body whole and incorrupt," and not only the body "but the vestments wherein the body lay were fresh, safe, and not consumed." *

The monks after this hid the body under a marble stone beneath the spot over which the shrine had been elevated, but it is presumed that it was removed thence by pious hands very shortly after, and buried under some steps, where only of late years its presence has been suspected.

* "Rites of Durham," p. 85.

DESTRUCTION AND RECONSTRUCTION. 31

> "Deep in Durham's Gothic shade
> His relics are in secret laid ;
> But none may know the place,
> Save of his holiest servants three,*
> Deep sworn to solemn secrecy,
> Who share that wondrous grace."

Lindisfarne Monastery had been left in the charge of one monk, whose mission was to watch the Danes and take charge of sacred vessels in the church. He remained concealed within the church when the Danes entered, heard them threaten to kill the monks when they returned, and contriving to escape to the Kyloe hills whither his brethren had fled, he recommended them not again to return.

The church was destroyed, and the monastic institute in Northumbria received its death-blow.

Meanwhile a war had been going on north of the Tweed, which was altering the geography, as it was changing the character of the British Isles.

The western Scots and their eastern neighbours the Picts had for ages amalgamated, and their royal houses had so intermarried, that, as an historian quaintly puts it, "hence arose a deadly feud between the two nations." Donald, who was King of the Scots and one of the lineal successors of Cornall, who had invited St

---

* Allusion to three monks of the Benedictine order who are supposed to know where the body actually lies ; but this is incorrect, for not three but all the Benedictine monks are told the secret, and may tell the secret if they please, for no oath binds them to it.

Columba over to Iona to preach the gospel to its Pictish neighbours, laid claim to the Pictish crown as direct heir to its deceased sovereign, but the claim was violently resisted by the Picts, who refused to listen to his pretensions, which were founded on hereditary right only, and informed him that, having by their own valour purchased their privilege to elect their own ruler, it was derogatory to their honour to accept a king merely on account of his blood pretensions. Suiting their action to their haughty message, they elected as sovereign a prince of their own race, thus declaring war to the Scottish Pretender.

In the many encounters which ensued, Donald, or Dungal, was not successful, and finally falling into the hands of the Picts, he was "butchered by them with inhuman cruelty," A.D. 842.*

It was clear that the Scots would not allow such a death to go unavenged, and Kenneth, the son of Alpin, who died in combat the same year (A.D. 842†), and who succeeded Donald, swore to revenge his father's death, just about the very time that Ingwar and Ubba were swearing to avenge the death of their father, Rednar Lodbrog.

He marched an army into the Pictish realm, and slew its Pictish king near Aberdeen, pursuing his

* "Chronica de Mailros," p. 16. Bannatyne Publication, 1835.
† *Ibid.*

conquest to the north with such celerity and success that before A.D. 866 the Picts were the subjects of the Scots, as the Northumbrians had become those of the Danes.

But besides Northumberland the old province of Bernicia contained counties north of the Tweed which extended to the Forth, and the contiguity of Bernicia and the Picts had engendered kindly relations between them, which in the hour of its need the Picts appealed to, and not in vain. Picts flying before the conquering Kenneth took refuge with the friendly Bernicians, who assisted them in resisting their Scottish enemy.

Kenneth, exasperated at this conduct of the Bernicians, and at the injuries which their soldiers—"armis ferocissimi"*—were able to inflict upon his undisciplined levies, resolved upon treating them like the Picts, whom he had determined to exterminate. Carrying his arms down the east coast, he swept all before him until he reached the Tweed at Berwick; then moving southwards, he conquered all the country which had formerly been Bernicia, inclusive of the monastery of Melrose, until he came to the province of Strathclyde.

When this was done—and the time had been well chosen, for the Northumbrian kingdom was the prey

---

* See Camden, speaking of the early Northumbrians.

of the Danes*—England had found its frontier on the Tweed and Scotland its limit on that river.

"The dissolution of the Pictish state is scarcely to be paralleled in history. Almost every memorial of its existence was destroyed, and the very language of its people lost for ever. Kenneth's rage and insatiable revenge for the death of his father being such that nothing less than the extirpation of the whole race could appease him, he spared neither age nor sex, and razed their cities to their foundations, passing the ploughshare over them, that every memorial of that people might be clean done out."†

It is singular to reflect that while Columba's disciple had begun his apostolic mission at the mouth of the Tweed, and Christianity in the north had risen on its banks, that river marked the limit of Kenneth's victory, of that Kenneth who was the lineal successor of Conall, Columba's patron.

Where Christianity had first displayed its standard, there rose the frontiers of "merry England;" and where the Scottish monk had fixed his home, there Scotland followed with her boundary.

No less remarkable is it that as the last North-

* "In the year that Kenneth, passing the mountains of Drumalbin, destroyed the monarchy of the Picts, these latter people are said to have been weakened by a great overthrow they had received from the Danish pirates; which overthrow paved the way to Kenneth's conquest."—Ridpath's "History of the Border."

† Hutchinson's "Antiquities of Durham," vol. i. p. 50.

umbrian king was dying a cruel death, as the Danes were asserting their rude supremacy, as the Scots were developing into a strong and haughty race, and as the monasteries first founded by the Anglo-Saxons within the "Patrimony of St Cuthbert" were being razed to the ground, Norham was the one "cell" or dependency within the original See of Lindisfarne that was not disturbed by the Danes, and dared peep its modest head above the storms of those fearful days.

Destined to be the vanguard of England in its political history, as it had been the vanguard of Christianity on its first invasion of northern English soil, Norham still can tell how races have gone down, how creeds have changed, how people have altered, but how, in the midst of all these revolutions, it has remained true to its founder and his noble mission, as it has been for ever loyal to English soil and king.

CHAPTER III.

SETTLEMENT OF GEOGRAPHICAL LIMITS.

875 to 1099.

Siward. "This way, my lord ; the castle's gently render'd :
The tyrant's people on both sides do fight ;
The noble thanes do bravely in the war ;
The day almost itself professes yours,
And little is to do."—*Shakespeare's "Macbeth."*

ANOTHER two centuries had elapsed. Saxon and Danes were gradually disappearing under the rule of those sturdy Norman barons who had laid hold of our island with so firm a grip. English and Scot were now in presence of one another, and about to fight for mastery across the river Tweed and all along its banks. William the Bastard had found his mate in Malcolm III. of Scotland.

The "Patrimony of St Cuthbert" had been restored to the Lindisfarne See, now permanently established at Durham; but the holy bishops of the earlier church had passed away, and the new men who succeeded them were warriors in the cause of wealth and power more than in that of religious progress. The age was an essentially fighting age, and bishops had to fight for their position. Lords paramount, judges, admirals, military commanders, and priests all at once, they were only next to the king in power, and the kings could not afford to mistrust them.

At this great juncture of English history Norham again appears in the front ranks; and on "that hill of immense height upon the river Tweed, quite at the extreme end of Northumberland," * a castle rises on which British hopes are to be centred, for its strength will awe the invading Scot, and peace may reign beneath its favouring protection.

In an old history of Newcastle-on-Tyne by Bourne, written in 1736 and dedicated to the then mayor, Walter Blackett, and his aldermen, Messrs Ellison, Ridley, Fenwick, Carr, and Clayton, all names still distinguished either in that capital of Northumberland or in the county, there is the following passage: —"From the year 875 to 1074 Northumberland had been in a desolate condition," and quoting Hollingshead, he goes on thus: "By the invasion of the Danes, the churches and monasteries throughout Northumberland were so wasted and ruined, that a man could scarcely find a church standing at this time in all the county; and as for those that remained they were all covered with broom or thatch; and as for any abbey or monastery there was not one left, neither did any man for the space of two hundred

* Collis quædam immensæ altitudinis . . . super Thueodam flumen in extremis Northumbriæ finibus.—" Reginald Dunelmi," p. 149, cap. 73.

years take care for the repairing or building up of anything in decay, so that the people of this county knew not what a monk meant, and if they saw any they wondered at the strangeness of the sight."

Perhaps these simple words convey a better account of the ravages, the plunder, the pillage, the burning, and the slaughter which ensued during this desolate period, than a more elaborate account of the doings in the days when the fight for political supremacy had its centre in the midland counties, and Northumberland was left in the charge, sometimes of an earl appointed by the English kings, and at others of the Scottish rulers as they happened to be victors in their endless encounters.

These earls, besides, had countless wrongs to be avenged, and every knight slain was a signal for further bloodshed. Reconciliations would take place when treachery had its play, and the dastardly acts were immediately punished by the wholesale butchery of hundreds of unoffending men and women. It seemed as if peace was never again to be known in the north of England. So tired were the Northumbrians of massacre and bloodshed, that when they heard in 1016 that Canute the Great, a man of still greater strength of will than any Danish commander of whom they had yet heard, was marching towards the north, they submitted "from need," says the

Saxon chronicle, and delivered hostages without striking a blow, together with their Earl Uchtred.

But the peace which ensued was only of two years' duration; for Uchtred having wrested the Lothians from the Scots during his governorship, the Scots in 1018 gave battle to his feeble brother and successor, Eadulf, at Carham-on-Tweed, twelve miles south-west of Norham, and so completely annihilated his army, that "a levy having been made of the whole population between the Tees and the Tweed, by far the greater part perished, including especially the older men, whose services on ordinary occasions would have been dispensed with. So overwhelming was the calamity that the venerable Bishop Aldhune died of grief, and Eadulf seems to have had no alternative but to agree to any terms which were offered to him."

This battle of Carham is interesting in the fact that from this time the Tweed became the politically recognized limit between the eastern marches of England and Scotland.

But the history of our Isles was now rushing to its development, and the Danes were to face a fiercer race even than their own. Their day of retribution was at hand. Canute, Harold, Hardicanute were gone, and Edward the Confessor was king. The old Saxon race was once more supreme—it was but the flickering of a light of which the fuel is burnt out.

The Earl of Northumberland in 1041 was Siward, —" a giant in stature, whose vigour of mind was equal to his bodily strength;" and legendary reports told how a bear had fallen in love with his mother, and Siward was the son of the bear. He was no monster himself, however; but while "a noble specimen of humanity" according to some, he was reputed so brave and decided that on hearing of a further Danish invasion, "the great men of the land, consulting with the king, did advise that the little devil Siward should be first exposed to the great devil," and thus all the land from Humber to Tweed was confided to his administration.

This "noble specimen of humanity," in the year 1054, "went into Scotland with a great army, both with a ship force and with a land force, and fought against the Scots, and put to flight King Macbeth, and slew all the chief men in the land, and carried thence much booty, such as no man before had obtained." That he was a very "devil" of a warrior is better established; for when he heard of his son's death at the head of his army, he inquired whether his death-wound was before or behind. "Before," was the reply. "Then I am more satisfied," said he; "no other death was fitting either for him or for me."*

---

* Shakespeare must have had this answer in mind when Rosse announcing Macbeth's death, Siward asks:

"Had he his hurts before?
Rosse. Ay, on the front.
Siward. Why then, God's soldier be he!
Had I as many sons as I have hairs
I would not wish them to a fairer death."

He died, however, of sickness at York; and so annoyed was he to find that his end was approaching far from the battle-field, that he exclaimed, "Shame on me that I did not die in one of the many battles I have fought, but am reserved to die with disgrace the death of a sick cow! Put on my armour, gird my sword by my side, place my helmet on my head, my shield in my left hand, and my battle-axe in my right, that at least I may die in a soldier's harness." Thus died a staunch old Northumbrian earl in the days of Edward the Confessor.

At his death Tosti, a son of the famous Earl Godwin, was made Earl of Northumberland, and the appointment stirred the blood of the northerners, who had not yet learned, and were not to learn for some centuries later, to look upon the south as part of a patriotic brotherhood, of which they were to hold the links if not the reins.

On the day of Tosti's arrival and his followers, the Northumbrian thanes first seized his Danish huscarls and put them to death; the next day they slew more than two hundred of his attendants; they broke open his treasury, carried off all that belonged to him, and then went to Harold in deputation, unanimously rejected his proposal to restore peace between them and Tosti, declared him outlawed, and chose Morcar as his successor.

The year 1066 had now arrived, and the Norman

William with his crowd of barons had landed on Anglo-Saxon soil.

Morcar, on hearing of the battle of Hastings (for he had not been present, though in London at the time), vowed "that he and his brother Edwin would fight together for Edgar Atheling" the rightful heir to Harold's throne, but William's movements were too rapid, and abandoning all idea of resistance they tendered to the Norman Conqueror their submission and their allegiance. They submitted, in the common sense words of the old Saxon chronicle, "for need when the most harm was done, and it was very unwise that they had not done so before."

Morcar and Edwin, however, were not restored to their honours, but carried off to France in the train of William, upon whom they had to dance "in honourable attendance."

The old Saxon pride revolted against this new position, and on their return to England they broke into open rebellion; but a greater affront had been offered to the English nation.

The most illustrious of the noble families of England, Earls of Mercia for generations, to which the Earldom of Northumberland had been added by the last Saxon king, the whole realm was likely to resent any insult offered to these brothers.

William I. had offered his daughter in marriage to Edwin, and the Norman barons made William retract his word, as "the earl was not good enough for the bastard's daughter," thus branding the whole English nation as an inferior people.

At once messages were sent all over the country to rouse the natives against their enemies. All joined in a firm league and bold conspiracy for the recovery of their ancient liberties, and the rebellion broke out with great violence in the provinces beyond the Humber. . . . "Many of the citizens lived in tents, disdaining the shelter of houses, as tending to enervate them."

But William was a man of genius besides a bold warrior, and with an unerring instinct he left the northern districts in the possession of the insurgents, until he had by means of the Bishop of Durham insured himself of an alliance with Malcolm, King of Scotland.

Though this was not actually done, Egelwin, Bishop of Durham, got Malcolm to withhold his aid to the insurgents, and the great rebellion collapsed as quickly as it had sprung up. William then understood how powerful a British ruler would be in the future with the Bishop of Durham, a priest on whom he could rely.

But the Danish massacres had still to be outdone, and the Norman name to be feared in the north as the Danes had been.

The first Norman Earl of Northumberland was

Robert de Comines, who arrived at Durham in 1069, on the 28th of January, and "so great was the terror inspired by his approach, that the first impulse of the people was to betake themselves to flight, leaving their houses and their property rather than subject themselves to the vengeance of the tyrannical Norman;" but a great fall of snow prevented this resolve, and a conspiracy was then formed to make away with Robert, so they "mutually pledged themselves to do this, or to perish in the attempt."

Passages like this show almost better than any description how reduced and desperate were the people who could afford to risk their lives for the purpose of murdering a man who was appointed to look after their welfare, and of whom they knew nothing.

The Bishop of Durham informed the new governor or earl of the people's intention, but he laughed it to scorn, and suffered his followers to commit any unlawful act they pleased.

At daybreak, however, on the morning following his arrival, a large body of Northumbrians appeared at the gates of Durham, and entering the streets "slew the earl's followers wherever they found them." The house where he lodged was set on fire, and St Cuthbert's Church was only preserved "by that saint's active interference." Comines perished in the fire, and but one of his followers escaped to tell the tale. Matters were assuming an ugly look. Cospatrick, the expatriated Earl of Northumberland, at the head of the discontented Saxons, marched upon York. Malet, the Sheriff of Yorkshire, earnestly appealed to William for reinforcements. The king marched to his relief in person, and surprising the insurgents by a quick march, "routed them with great slaughter, and effectually dispersed them."

He then returned to Winchester in triumph, and to prepare his revenge for Comines' death. He leisurely organized an expedition against the bishoprick of Durham, which never reached Durham owing to a dense fog, but was soon employed against the Danes.

The spirit of William being fully roused, he marched into Northumberland, and spent the whole winter laying waste the country, slaughtering the inhabitants, and inflicting on them without intermission every sort of evil.

"It was dreadful to behold human corpses, rotting in the houses, streets, and highways, reeking with putrefaction, swarming with worms, and contaminating the air with deadly exhalations: for all the people being cut off by the sword or by famine, there were none left to bury them."

"In consequence of the ravages of the Normans, so severe a famine prevailed throughout the kingdom, but chiefly in Northumberland and the adjacent provinces, that men were driven to feed on the carcases of horses, dogs, and cats, and even of human flesh."

It is consoling to hear, after so terrible an account, that on his death-bed William allowed that he had " become, alas! the barbarous murderer of thousands upon thousands, both old and young," thus expressing, as well as his rude nature allowed, some regret for the merciless revenge he had taken on those who had called upon the Danes under Sweyne to come and help them against the Norman invader.

Historians of the present day are wont to sing the praises of William and his barons, because they brought with them institutions which constitute the ground-work upon which our modern legal system is founded, and also because the greater portion of the British nobility who claim a genuine ancestry, trace their origin back to some Norman companion of the bastard William; but the fact remains that a more merciless set of ruffians never trod upon British soil, and a more annihilating horde of robbers never trampled on any country. The Romans had left behind them memories of benefits conferred, and of a rule both wise and just though stern; the Danes, though savage, spoke a language akin to our own, and contrived when not bent on destruction to ingratiate themselves with the people, to amalgamate with them, and to form a mixed race which gave promise of strength of power and of unity, but the Normans spoke a jargon which alarmed as much as it reminded the vanquished of their defeat. The insolent and overbearing manner of the conquerors offended as it naturally created resentment, and in the end the native element was trodden down and crushed never to rise again.*

It was not so in Scotland, and from the first the Norman barons had to learn that "to the Tweed and no step further" was to be their guiding rule.

Malcolm Cean Mor, the elder of the two sons of Duncan, by a sister of Siward, Earl of Northumberland, refused to recognise William as the legitimate king of England.

Born in 1024, he sought Siward's protection in 1039 on the assassination of his father by Macbeth, and was placed for a time under the care of Edward the Confessor at his Court in London, where he became acquainted with Edgar Atheling and his beautiful sister Margaret.

* "The minds of men were froward and inclined to quarrels and warfare: they were overwhelmed in excess and sensuality; vanity, lust, and intemperance reigned everywhere. (Malmesbury.)

"Even the king's servants, following him in his journeys, used to harass and plunder the country as their wickedness instigated, and many of them were so extravagant in their barbarity, that what they could not eat or drink in their quarters, they either obliged the people to carry to market and sell for their emolument, or they threw it into the fire. At their departure they frequently washed their horses' heels with the wine left undrunk, or wasted

In 1054 he accompanied his cousin Robert, the son of Siward, into Scotland, where they forced Macbeth to give up the Lothians, which country was then placed under his rule by Siward; and in 1056, with the further assistance of Siward, he marched north to Lumphanan in Aberdeenshire. There he overtook and slew Macbeth, and in the following spring defeated Lulach, Macbeth's stepson, at Essie in Strathbogie, thus putting an end to all resistance against him.

Crowned at Scone in 1057, he paid a visit of gratitude to Edward the Confessor in 1059, ravaged Northumberland in 1061, because Tostig had proved "false to his friendship," and in 1066 received at his Court the fugitive remnants of Saxon royalty.

Boece tells how a storm drove the fleet, with Harold's widow and Edgar Atheling and his sisters Margaret and Christina, into the Firth of Forth, and how the road wherein they sought shelter took the name of Margaret's Hope, and still is called so;* how

it on the ground. As for outrages committed on the persons of subjects, both men and women, they went to the utmost length of licentiousness and cruelty. For these reasons, when they heard the king was coming, everybody quitted their houses and fled with their effects." (Malmesbury.)

* "When this Edgar Athelinge,
That of law should have been king,
The kingdom saw distroubled so,
Of counsel with his sisters two.

Malcolm, then residing at Dunfermline, "sent envoys to enquire of what lineage and country the strangers were—

> "Sed vos qui tandem, quibus aut venistis ab oris,
> Quove tenetis iter?"

and found to his dismay that they were of the line of the Confessor, his benefactor; how he at once offered them hospitality, receiving them with all the honour due to their rank, to his old affection for the family, and to the promise once made to him by Edward that Margaret should be his bride.

Malcolm's love and admiration for this excellent princess forms almost a romance in those days of

> A ship he got and took the sea,
> For to pass again thought he,
> And arrive in the empire
> Whereof the Lord was his good sire.
> And as they were on the sea land,
> The wind askant was then blowing,
> And all the weather on their journey
> Was to their purpose all contrary,
> That perforce as the wind them moved,
> Came in the Firth which them behoved,
> And in St Margaret's Hope by leave
> Of proper need they did arrive.
> In this manner Saint Margaret,
> In the empire upon which,
> Came to be a Scottish name
> In King Malcolm's reign."

Wyntoun, quoted in the original Saxon in the Registrum de Dunfermline, published by the Bannatyne Club.

sword and battle. So great was his respect and his admiration that Turgot, who had accompanied her on the journey, says: "The king liked and disliked whatever she did, and, unable to read, was in the habit of kissing her missals and prayer-books, and having them ornamented with gold and precious stones."

She brought with her the civilizing influences of the south, and soon regenerated a court which had not known before the blessings of learning and of education.

This princess is reputed to have been so fond of her old country that she was wont to pay the ransom of her Saxon countrymen out of her own means when she found them in bondage in Scotland. Her resignation to the will of God, on hearing of the death of her husband and eldest son near Alnwick, is beautifully depicted in the following prayer which she is said to have offered up when the news was broken to her: "Praise and blessing to thee, Almighty God, that thou hast been pleased to make me endure so bitter an anguish in the hour of my departure, thereby I trust to purify me in some measure from the corruption of my sins."

Then, as if the blow had been too much, the saintly queen dropped down dead.

Her daughter married Henry I., thereby restoring a little English blood to the kings of England.

She tamed her husband to the degree of making him act as her interpreter with the Scotch clergy who had not given up their views about the keeping of Easter, and Sir Walter Scott, in his interesting preface to "Border Antiquities," remarks that this circumstance proves not only "that Malcolm Canmore understood both Saxon and Celtic" (which by the way is natural, considering that he had been educated at the Confessor's court), but "establishes the fact that the Lowland Scotch had not yet spread generally through the Celtic tribes, though it did so afterwards."

Of course Malcolm espoused the cause of his brother-in-law Edgar, and invaded England with the assistance of Danes and the Northumbrian nobles led by Gospatrick.* His progress, as we have seen, was stopped by the craftiness or statesmanship of William, who, through the Bishop of Durham, arrested Malcolm's progress by the information that Gospatrick might prove a traitor. Of this fact he soon became aware, for turning his march into England from east to west, he reached the eastern parts of the Durham diocese,

* This great earl was the son and heir of Maldred, who married Algetha, daughter and heir of Uchtred, Earl of Northumberland, by Algiva, daughter of King Ethelred of England. Maldred was son of Crinan, one of the greatest and most opulent families in the north of England. From him in direct male line are descended the Nevilles, the most illustrious family in antiquity, and the representative of which is now the Earl of Abergavenny. According to Dugdale, he died at Norham, and was buried in the porch of the church there.

after wasting Teesdale and defeating a Norman army at Hinderskill, when he heard that Gospatrick was laying waste his own county of Cumberland, in King William's interest, whereupon "he spared neither age nor sex," and led captive into Scotland so many young men and women that "for many years they were to be found in every Scottish village, nay, in every Scottish hovel."

In 1072, William tried to retaliate by invading Scotland both by land and by sea, but he had soon to sue for peace at Abernethy.

In 1079, Gospatrick, having betrayed William, was deprived of his earldom of Northumberland, and becoming reconciled with Malcolm, was created by him Earl of Dunbar.

His first step was to induce Malcolm to invade England, which that sovereign agreed to do, and penetrated through Northumberland to the Tyne.

In 1080, the English invaded Scotland under Robert, but were obliged to retreat.

It was then that Newcastle was built to check the incursions of the Scots.

As the Chronicle of Mailros relates in charmingly simple language : " The Conqueror sent his son Robert Courtois or Courtehose (viz., of the short breeches) against Malcolm in 1080, who, having done nothing, upon his return built the New Castle upon the river Tyne."

The town had, previously to this time, been called Monkchester, or Monks' defence, and it only lost that name when the castle was built.

At last the old Scottish king, after having "on five occasions afflicted Northumberland with dreadful ravages and carried off its wretched inhabitants into slavery," and having under William Rufus advanced to Chester-le-Street, "slaughtering multitudes of human beings and burning their dwellings," was induced by "hostages sent to him in Scotland" to obey William's summons to Gloucester; but not being able "either to obtain an audience of the king, or the performance of certain stipulations" connected with the cession of Carlisle, in a fit of temper he returned to Scotland, and assembling his troops, resolved on invading England once more.

Robert, Earl of Northumberland, a son of Roger de Mowbray, a companion-in-arms of William, of whom Ordericus Vitalis says that "he was bold and crafty of disposition, and inflated with empty pride," "lay in wait for him with his men, and he was killed by Morel of Bamburgh,* the earl's deputy," A.D. 1092.

---

* In 1095, finding Bamburgh, to which he had laid siege almost impregnable, William Rufus erected another fort called "Malvoisin," a French word for bad neighbour, immediately opposite, and drew off with his main army to Alnwick, "the better to engage the rebel Mowbray." Mowbray, after holding secret communication with his friends at Newcastle, found out that Rufus had left, and started to take possession; but, on arriving before Newcastle, he

The death of this old warrior king, whose body was "carried in a cart by two countrymen to Tynemouth, and there interred," was the signal for the rise and rapid growth of the See of Durham, which was to play so important a part in the history of the north during the centuries that followed.

In 1093, William de Carilepho, "who was in very high favour with the king," restored to the see the lands which the king had severed from it, and re-established "the Patrimony of St Cuthbert," which comprised Ubbanford, or Norham as it was then called, while he began, from plans which he had brought over from France, the present Cathedral of Durham. The wars with Malcolm and the Scottish invasions had shown the necessity of fortresses on the frontiers for the purposes of defence. New Castle was being built, but other lines of defence were necessary to protect the lands above Tyne.

found the gates were shut, and was refused entrance, whereupon he hurried to Tynemouth; his movements, however, having been watched by the king's army, he was overtaken and made prisoner. His wife, meanwhile, and Morel defended Bamburgh against every assault, and it was only on finding that Mowbray had been captured that they at last capitulated. Rufus, in reward of the good defence made by Lady Mowbray and by Morel, pardoned all three.

Camden says: "After Mowbray's flight, the castle was stoutly maintained by Morel till the earl himself was by the king's order brought within view of the fort, and threatened with the having his eyes put out, whereupon it was immediately surrendered." —"Britannia," vol. i. p. 1097.

Bishop Walcher, who preceded Carilepho, had been the first to obtain with the Earldom of Northumberland the privilege of uniting the civil with the ecclesiastic power in his see, and the people had rebelled against the "palatine jurisdiction." To the cry of "short red, good red, slea ye the bishoppe," he was brutally pierced to the heart with a lance.

Carilepho had preferred at one time Duke Robert to William Rufus, and had only returned to favour by a service rendered to the king's troops in Normandy.

In future none but reliable friends of the king must be selected for the See of Durham, as they would be the king's lieutenants in the palatinate which was outside the jurisdiction of Northumberland, and would have to protect the king's frontier which began on the Tweed.

"Bishop Carilepho had displayed a military standard, in consequence of his palatine jurisdiction similar to that of a sovereign prince, called the banner of St Cuthbert, which was carried with the troops into Scotland. The expedition might furnish an idea that a fortress at Norham would prove a barrier of the utmost consequence to the possessions of the church and to the protection of Northumberland."[*]

The idea had occurred before, but Malcolm's

[*] Hutchinson, vol. iii, p. 393.

constant invasions had prevented any possibility of building. Now, indeed, that the village and its neighbourhood had reverted to the church, and the Bishop of Durham had become the king's representative, both ecclesiastic, civil, and military, on the borders, the first military act to be performed was the construction of a fortress on the high cliff that overhangs the Tweed from the English side.

In 1099 Ralph de Flambard was consecrated Bishop of Durham. "The convulsions of the State and the bishop's adversity prevented him executing a plan which he had conceived on his obtaining the See, for he was of a bold and enterprising spirit, and had a genius for military affairs." Berwick was not yet to be a fort. It had been given to the See of Durham, but "its chief consequence was in maritime affairs." Of these little is heard as compared with the warfares on land, and surely that had been such in the latter years of the century that a fortress at Norham must have appeared of the greatest consequence to the frontier.

Already the Scots on the hills opposite, whereon Ladykirk now stands, had apparently constructed a camp.* It was known by the name of Monugenede,† and overhung a deep pool called Padduwell ‡ (the modern Pedwell), which, according to Reginald of

* Vallata collis. † Quæ Monugenede dicta.
‡ Qui Padduwell dicitur.

Durham's account, was celebrated on account of the following story which he relates.

"There is a village called Northam, close on the limits of Lothian, situated on the river Tweed at the extreme end of Northumberland, which was known even before the time of St Cuthbert. In its immediate vicinity there is a hill of immense height and great breadth, . . . where the following occurred.

"In the above named village there is an old church dedicated to St Cuthbert, and youths were wont to repair to it for study, some moved by the love of knowledge, others from fear of their masters' severity.

"One boy called Haldene, belonging to the latter category, ruminated on one occasion how he could avoid both his lessons in the church and the stripes.

"So he bethought himself that if he could take the key of the church and quickly throw it into the Tweed, no one would discover the theft. He then went beneath the hill of immense height which is called Munigenede, where the water is said to be extremely deep, and goes by the name of Padduwel (Pedwell), and quickly threw the key into the river, then ran away so that no officious or curious person should stop him.

. . . . .

"Towards evening the master asked for the key, but he was told it could not be found. Greatly perturbed in mind, the master knew not what to do, for the doors were of brass and iron, of great weight and strength of metal, but in the night St Cuthbert appeared to him and seriously reprehended him for not officiating in his church as usual. The master pleaded the loss of the key. The saint then said : Go to-morrow early in the morning to the Pedwell site on the Tweed, and tell the fishermen you will give them any price they ask for the first fish they catch.

"This was done, but the fishermen had decided among themselves that for the love of St Cuthbert, in accordance with the old custom they would make a present of the first fish to the priest.

"A salmon of very large size was first caught, holding within its jaws something which it could neither hide nor swallow. Its stomach was distended and inflated. Full of confidence in St Cuthbert, the priest put his hand in the jaws of the fish, and there he found hanging to the upper jaw the key of his church which he had lost." *

It was resolved to build a fort on Norham Hill, and in 1121 the work began.

* A similar story is told about a ring lost over the parapet of the old bridge at Newcastle, and related in the Survey of Newcastle in 1649.

"There was a strange accident upon the bridge happened to an alderman of Newcastle, looking over the bridge into the river, with his hands over : his gould ring fell off his finger into the water, which was given for lost. It chanced that one of his servants bought a salmon in the market, opening the belly of the fish, found his master's ring in the guts."

Up to this time the "Patrimony of St Cuthbert," the land of Aidan, had not required any works to protect its limits against the foe. The only fortresses in its neighbourhood had been Wark, further up the Tweed, and Bamborough on the East Coast, but with the Normans, castles of defence became the order of the day, and as Norham was being planned, New Castle and Carlisle were being built.

With the building of Norham, too, new geographical limits were being formed within the kingdom. The united Bernicia and Deira of King Oswald, which extended to the Tees from the Forth, became the Earldom of Northumberland at the Danish invasion, with its limits from the Tweed to the Tees; and now, in 1121, the Northumberland of the present day, from Tyne to Tweed, was settling within its boundaries, and Norham was being shaped into the queen of Border fortresses upon the English soil of Northumberland.*

* "So late as the reign of Edward I. the palatinate of Durham was still regarded as within the county of Northumberland." — Hodgson, Part i. p. 202.

CHAPTER IV.

FLAMBARD.

1099—1128.

"Brave men were living before Agamemnon
 And since, exceeding valorous and sage:
 A good deal like him, too, though quite the same none;
 But then they shone not on the poet's page,
 And so have been forgotten."—*Byron.*

SHORTLY before the battle of Hastings, a family of mean occupations and no convictions except a decided wish to better themselves by robbing those who set them the example of plunder, had their number increased by the birth of a son in some dull town of Normandy.

This offspring "from the dregs of the people"* was brought up as the sons of the poor in those days were all brought up—that is, in a manner that so much resembled the condition of wild beasts that the severity of the masters whom they were compelled to serve as slaves became a civilizing boon.

Ralph, who subsequently was called Flambard, probably from his having been a torch-bearer to some Norman of birth, appears to have been of a quick,

* Lord Lyttleton's "History of Henry II."

bold, and enterprizing disposition, besides possessing an agreeable face and winning manners. These qualities constituted his stock-in-trade, and while they procured him bread in his youth, they ensured his advancement in after life.

England being for many years after its conquest by William the favourite plundering resort of his knights and barons, Flambard came over in the suite of one of these, and being endowed with "great subtlety of genius, ready wit, and eloquence," soon established a claim to reward.

He was raised from the condition of a servant to be dean of the collegiate church of Christ Church or Twynham, in Hants,[*] by Mauritius, Bishop of London, notwithstanding that "he had scarce any learning, and not so much as an external show of religion."

This post, however, was too peaceable for a nature so active, and "the depravity of his principles," with which he is charged by Godwin in the Anglo-Saxon Chronicles, required the field of London and the court for the gratification of his passions.

He applied to his patron Mauritius for the deanery of London, but being refused this lucrative post, he was made chaplain to King Rufus by way of compensation, and from this moment his rise was rapid.

"Fertile in the invention for ways and means of

[*] "Qui Randulphus antea fuerat Decanus in Ecclesia Christi de Twynham."—Dugdale's "Monasticon," vol. vii., p. 303.

raising money, with a remorseless insensibility to the complaints of the people, and a daring contempt of the resentment of the nobles,"* no wonder he became a favourite of the king, who, according to a French historian,† "possessed all the vices of his father without any of his qualities: who was neither religious nor temperate, and who, on causing fifty English gentlemen to go through the ordeal of fire on suspicion of hunting without leave, swore by St Luke's face, on hearing that they all had passed through the ordeal in safety, that he could never believe in God's justice since such offenders were thus protected by Providence."

So useful a chaplain was not long before he was transferred to positions where he could devise further exactions and taxes for the benefit of his sovereign, and he was made Surveyor of the King's Homages, which gave the tenants of the crown a taste of his extortions.

Finally he was made "Chief Justiciary and Procurator-General," under which employments he conducted himself so oppressively and with such injustice that he incurred a general odium.

London had by this time become too hot for him, and his own savings had accumulated to the extent that he bribed Rufus in the sum of £1000, which at that time represented about £3000 of our present

* Lord Lyttleton's "History of Henry II." † Rapin.

money, to confer upon him the See of Durham, which had been vacant three years, during which time, by advice of Flambard and contrary to old usages, the temporalities of the see had reverted to the crown.

On the 5th of June 1099 Ralph Flambard was consecrated Bishop of Durham by Thomas, Archbishop of York, at St Paul's Church in London, "without, as was wont, declaring his submission to the archiepiscopal jurisdiction," and at once proceeded to Durham with private recommendations from the king, among which was that of strengthening his diocese by a chain of fortified castles, which, in case of need, would help the king to gain time and bring up his forces.

He had not been much over a year at Durham, however, during which time he had resolved on strengthening Durham and on building a castle of defence at Norham, when news reached him of his friend's death in the new forest, shot by the willing arrow of Sir Walter Tyrrell.

The first act of Henry I., by way of showing his desire to conciliate a rebellious people, was to commit the hated minister of the late king to prison, and on the 14th of September 1100, by the advice of the great council of the kingdom, Flambard was sent a close prisoner to the Tower of London, with an allowance of two shillings a day from the king, under the custody of William de Magnaville.

His facetious humour and wit prevailed upon his goalers to connive at his escape; and "one day, the 4th of February 1101, having feasted them sumptuously and left them all drunk about him, he fastened a rope to the pillar in the centre of his window, and taking with him his pastoral staff, he descended to some friends who waited for him at the foot of the Tower, his hands, for want of gloves, being excoriated to the bone by the passing of the cord. Horses being ready for him he fled with all speed with a few faithful followers. His steward met him upon the road with his treasure, and immediately taking shipping, he arrived safe in Normandy."

Repairing at once to the court of Duke Robert, he prevailed on him to allow him to administer to the, bishopric of Luxemburg during the minority of his son, and this he did for the space of three years. At the end of this time he hit upon a plan for recovering his more lucrative See of Durham, which was certainly a bold stroke of policy. He advised Duke Robert to invade England. He urged upon him his rights and claims to a throne which Henry had usurped, and told him that what with his knowledge of the country and the information he received, together with the promises he had of support, the duke would be sure of success. He meanwhile allowed it to transpire that the duke was raising a powerful army for such an invasion, and gave out that the only way of arresting his progress might be by offering him such a sum of money as he could accept, and by the grant of a free pardon and the restoration of their honours and estates to those who had aided him.

On the 19th of July 1104, the duke, attended by the bishop and a powerful army, was setting out on the projected expedition, when "by an interposition of the nobles on both sides, and a considerable sum of money given by King Henry to discharge the expenses of Duke Robert's equipment, a peace was concluded, and all those who had aided the duke received the king's pardon, and were restored to their honours and estates."

Flambard returned to London and to his See of Durham, and his first care was to endeavour to gain the king's favour by the same means which he had found so successful with his predecessor—namely, at the expense of the people. But times were changed, and gifts alone to the king and his surroundings were not sufficient to gain royal approval.

Henry I., by a succession of charters, defined the limits of the Diocese of Durham, the rights and privileges within the Patrimony of St Cuthbert, and the extent to which the Northumbrians could hunt and cut wood in the forests of St Cuthbert between Tyne and Tweed: "for one penny, an annual load of fuel wood as one cart would carry," and "for a silver piece, the largest tree in the woods annually for shipbuilding."

Finding that he had a master, Flambard applied himself henceforth by numerous works of utility to add to the power and magnificence of his bishopric. He carried up the walls of Durham Church to the roof, and enlarged the common hall of its adjoining monastery. He built the wall from the church to the castle so as to strengthen the already strong natural position of the town; he fortified the castle with a moat, and strengthened the banks of the river, over which he threw the arched bridge of stone which is now known as Framwellgate bridge. He founded, in 1112, the hospital of Kepier, near Durham, and endowed it; when he had provided for his own neighbourhood he remembered his promise to Rufus, and armed with plans which he had brought with him from Normandy he journeyed to the Tweed, where at Northam, or Norham, his northern home, he gave orders for the construction of the castle.

From the very earliest times, the country which is watered by the river Tweed was made use of for strategical purposes, and remains of Roman earthworks still exist all along the banks of Tweed, from Berwick to Melrose, at the foot of the Eildon Hills (which is supposed to have been the Trimontium, and capital town of the Selgovæ tribes—a very proper appellation for a town situated at the foot of three peaks). All these camps may date about the year A.D. 80, when Julius Agricola proceeded northwards to the estuary of the Tay, and built that chain of forts which extended from the Forth to the Clyde. Their peculiar formation can be traced at Horncliffe, at Tillmouth, at Wark, near Coldstream, at Carham, and further up the river, each of these places being singularly well adapted either for crossing the river or for watching the approach of an enemy.

To the south of Norham Castle * there is a broad and level platform, defended by ravines, upon which the Archæological Institute have discovered remains of a Roman camp, and the traces of banks and ditches which the besiegers of Norham have raised or dug. But on the high steep rock whereon the castle is built there are no Roman remains, and there is no mention that I can find of any Roman or other camp having ever been constructed there.

* Camden in his "Britannia" says,—"Twede, increased by Till, runs now in a larger stream by Norham, or Northam, which was formerly called Ubbanford. The town belongs to the Bishop of Durham; for Bishop Egfrid, who was a mighty benefactor to the See of Lindisfarne, built it and the church, and his successor Ralph erected the castle on the top of a steep rock, and moated it round, for the better security of this part of his diocese against the frequent incursions of the Scottish moss-troopers. On the outmost wall, and the largest in circuit, are placed several turrets on a canton towards the river, within which there is a second enclosure much stronger than the former, and in the middle of that again

In Saxon days there were two well-known fords: one at Carham and the other at Norham. The latter was the less practicable of the two and the least used, but it was especially the resort of the Lindisfarne friars, and so much so that one historian, whom Hutchinson has followed, declares it to have been the original see offered to Aidan by King Oswald.

The early Saxon kings selected their strongholds rather in places which were either inaccessible from the sea, or on the steep side of mountains. Thus Yevering Bell, a spur of the Cheviot range twelve miles south of Norham, shows even now remains of earthworks which go back to the days of Deira and Bernicia, while Bamborough was the first and only fortress which the Saxons bequeathed to their successors in the country north of Tyne. The Danes in their constant struggles against the Anglo-Saxons, and indeed against each other, had no other idea than to burn and destroy, and whatever they left of a defensive character was removed by the Normans to make way for buildings of their own. This remark applies almost equally to our cathedral churches, which, with the exception of a very small number,

rises a high keep. But the well-established peace of our times has made these forts to be long neglected, notwithstanding they are placed upon the very Borders. Under the castle, on a level westward, lies the town and church wherein was buried Ceolwulph, King of Northumberland, to whom Venerable Bede dedicated his books of the Ecclesiastical History of England."

were rebuilt from their foundations either on the same site, such as at York and Canterbury, or near the old one, as at Winchester, or in another place, as at Norwich and Peterborough.

Even the castles for defence which were built in the time of William the Conqueror and of his son William II., did not satisfy the architects of the reigns of Henry I. and Richard I. and Henry II.

Thus even such early Norman keeps as Newcastle-on-Tyne, Dover, Carlisle, Norwich, and Richmond, though begun at the end of the eleventh, were added to or altered or completed in a manner different to the original designs in the twelfth century.

Gundulph's or St Leonard's Tower at Malling in Kent, and the Tower of London, appear alone to subsist as genuine specimens of the workmanship of the eleventh century, and it must be allowed it is but very rude masonry.

The art had improved, however, in 1121, when once more the little village awoke from its summer drowsiness, and heard all at once that the Courts of Justice of the Palatinate were to hold their sittings within its rural limits, and that the "magnificent" Bishop Flambard had given orders for the construction of a castle on the "steep rock" which guards the entrance, so as to put an end to the predatory incursions of robbers and the sudden irruptions of the Scotch.*

* "Ut inde latronum incursus inhiberet et Scottorum irrup-

This rock hung perpendicularly to the river which flows smoothly at its feet, both on the north and eastern sides of the ridge, of which it is the spur, and afforded a natural strength to any fortress built on its summit which needed but an outward wall and keep to render the place almost impregnable if well garrisoned.*

To the south a forest of trees covered all the tract of country which lies between the castle and Berwick by Horncliffe, Longridge, and Ord, and to the west at the foot of the rock lay the village itself.

The excitement was enhanced by the prospect of privileges to be granted and work to be obtained.

Masons in great numbers flocked to the village from all parts of Northumberland, and soon the old keep, of which the foundations alone remain,† began

tiones, condidit castellum in excelso preruptærup is super Tuedam flumen. Ibi enim utpote in confinio regni Anglorum et Scottorum creber predantibus ante patebat excursus nullo ibidem, quo hujus modi impetus repellerentur, præsidio locato." — Symeon of Durham.

* "The castle stands upon a rocky platform, the south-western extremity of a cliff which forms the river bank for a considerable distance.

"A deep ravine cuts off the higher ground to the north-east, and is joined by a less marked depression, which, deepened by art, sweeps round and forms the southern defences until it opens upon the steep slope which descends to the river and forms the north and north-western front of the castle. Beyond this ditch was the approach from the village of Norham."—" Norham Castle," by C. F. Clark. Archæological Journal, Dec. 1876.

† " Flambard's masonry may be distinctly traced in the south-

to rise and shape itself into a massive square tower, with passages for communication between one part of the building and another in the thickness of the walls.

When this was done, probably all was finished that Flambard ever ordered, and certainly all that he ever saw, for in 1128 he was seized with a lingering disease.

When he found that death was threatening, he had himself carried into the church, and resting on the altar, with all his clergy around him, he made a public confession of all his faults, restored to monasteries the lands and effects he had appropriated to his own use, and made his will bequeathing all his money to the poor.

He then died with the consoling belief that having done all the mischief he could during a lifetime, he repaired all this harm by giving away at the last to the poor what he knew he could no longer enjoy.

There is a grim humour in this last act of his life which well harmonizes with the rest of his existence,

---

east corner and the whole east side of the tower. About thirty feet of the south side also are of his workmanship. His buttresses are flat, without stages, and his masonry is excellent. That his roof was ridged is proved by a chevron moulding within.

"In the southern wall the windows of Flambard's period are extremely narrow without, but flanning widely within."—D. Raine's "History of North Durham," p. 229.

and as if the last ray of wit was to have a practical character, King Henry I. constituted himself the heir of the bishop's ill-begotten wealth, and the poor were forgotten.

For all that, Flambard remains a character in history. His indomitable pluck and strength of will, his knowledge of human failings, his perseverance, his magnificence, his diplomacy mark him for ever as one of the greatest prelates of this realm, if indeed we cannot give him a place among its worthiest.

Shortly after Norham Castle had been commenced, Robert, a captain in King Edgar of Scotland's armies, presumed, as Flambard considered it, to erect a castle for himself on the Scotch side of the Tweed, probably on the "Monugenede" or Ladykirk Bank, which almost faces Norham Castle.

History does not tell whether this Captain Robert intended his castle for aggressive purposes, or for a home which he could defend if need be, but the bishop looked upon the construction as a menace to his newly erected stronghold. Without consulting King Henry, he levied an army in the Palatinate, and crossing the Tweed marched against the captain, whom he made prisoner.

Edgar was in London at the time, but on hearing of this trespass upon his territory, he hurried back, obtained the release of his subject, and retaliated by taking possession of Berwick,* but at his death, his son Alexander restored Berwick to the Patrimony of St Cuthbert, and gave it besides most of the Scotch territory which lies now between Norham and Aytoun, including Swinton, which is mentioned by name in his charter 1123, and of which the Sheriff "*Vice comes*" was Arnulf, whom the king calls " miles meus," my soldier, as mentioned in an article on his family by Mr Archibald Campbell Swinton of Kimmerghame, the present representative of that ilk, published in the proceedings of the Berwickshire Naturalists' Club for the year 1877.

It was about this time that the celebrated abbeys of Kelso, Jedburgh, Dryburgh, Coldingham, and Tyningham received their splendid architectural envelope, although their foundations went back to a much earlier age. †

* "Before Berwick became the unhappy subject of contention and war, it carried on the most extensive commerce of any port on the eastern coast of the island," and in the chronicles of Lanercost, Berwick is described as a city of such populousness and commerce, that it might fully be styled a second Alexandria, whose riches were the sea, and the waters its walls. In those days the citizens being very wealthy and devout to God, gave great alms, and instituted an order of friars of the Benedictine order.

"Ipsa civitas quondam adeo populosa ac negotiosa extiterat quod merito altera Alexandria dici poterat cujus divitiæ mare et aquæ muri ejus. Illis diebus cives præ potentes effecti et Deo devoti largas erogabant cleemosynas, &c.—Lanercost, folio 207, A.D. 1296.

This was however subsequently to the foundation of Norham.

† Although the Christian missionaries came originally from the

In 1113, while Roxburgh was in the height of its prosperity (and indeed not a house, not a trace now remains of its ever having been of importance), Earl David, heir-presumptive of the crown of Scotland, brought a little colony of thirteen reformed Benedictine monks from Tiron in France to his forest castle of Selkirk ; but the French monks, not liking the banks of the Ettrick, they obtained from David on his accession, permission to establish themselves at "the Church of the Blessed Virgin, on the bank of the Tweed beside Roxburgh, in the place called Calkon," and the translation took place in 1126.

In 1159 Malcolm IV. granted to it the charter which is described in the preface to "Registrum de Kelso" as "the most remarkable of Scotch charters," as "still preserved at Floors," as "carefully and even handsomely written," and as giving one "a favourable idea of the art of miniature as practised in the abbey."

But it has an additional advantage, one of immense importance to art in Scotland. The charter gives illuminated portraits of King David I., its founder, and of the "maiden Malcolm IV., his grandson."

The decay of the abbey dates with that of Norham,

Celtic Iona, yet the large foundations of Lindisfarne, Hexham, Melrose, Coldingham, Jedburgh, and others on the Borders were endowed by Saxon magnificence and filled with Saxon monks, who disseminated their language along with their religion through such tribes as still used the British or Celtic tongue."—Sir W. Scott's "Antiquities of the Borders," p. xxxvii.

as its building dates from that of the castle. In 1545 the church was converted into a fortress by the Earl of Hertford during his ferocious expedition against the Scots. Fnding that the Tweed "rose too suddenly," and that "the taking down of so great and superfluous buildings of stone would take at the leaste two moneths," he resolved "to rase and deface the house of Kelso, so as the enemye shall have lytell commoditie of the same," adding, "to-morrow we intend to send a good band of horsemen to Melrose and Dryburgh to burn the same," and to "march to Jedburgh to burn the same."

From that time to within quite lately the abbey has not been repaired, but its glorious old ruins, rising proudly on the lovely bank of Tweed, contrast most singularly with the modern aspect of the town of Kelso, if they don't tell that even in their shattered condition they have fared better than the oft-destroyed dwellings of the peaceful inhabitants of the border town.

The monastery of Dryburgh was founded by Hugh de Moreville, who came from Cumberland "in the year 1150 for monks of the Premonstratensian order or white canons, on the feast of St Martin," November 10.

These monks were dressed in white cassocks, long white cloaks, and a square bonnet or hat of white felt, and wore breeches and shoes, but no shirt. Although sworn to poverty, they attracted the attention of

David I. by their piety, and they soon became a rich order, and built a beautiful abbey, which was, however, destroyed in 1544 by Sir George Bowes, captain of Norham, of whom we shall hear more later, and who with "his company, Sir Brian Layton, Henry Eury, Liell Gray, porter, and the garrison of Berwick, together with John Carre, captain of Wark, Thomas Beamond, George Selby, Launcelot Carleton, and their companies, to the number of seven hundred men, rode into Scotland, upon the water of Tweide, to a town called Dryburgh, with an abbey in the same, which was a pretty town and well builded, and they burnt the same town and abbey, saving the church, with a great substance of corn, and got very much spoilage and insicht gear, and brought away a hundred nolte, sixty nags, a hundred sheep, and they tarried so long at the said burning and spoilage that it was Saturday at eight of the clock at night or they come home."*

The abbey was never fully rebuilt after this. In 1606 it was erected into the "temporal lordship" of Cardross, "the samyn monasteries and superstitions thereof being now abolisht," and Sir Walter Scott has recorded his regret that it never came into his hands through his father not purchasing it.

"The ancient patrimony was sold for a trifle (£5500), and my father, who might have purchased

---

* The complete MS. appears in "Reprints of Rare Tracts," edited by W. A. Richardson, Newcastle, in 1847. Vol. iv., Historical.

it with ease, was dissuaded by my grandfather, . . . and thus we have nothing left of Dryburgh, although my father's maternal inheritance, but the right of stretching our bones, where mine may perhaps be laid ere any eye but my own glances over these pages."*

Sir Walter Scott was buried at Dryburgh, and well may it be said that no fitter place could be found for the sepulture of Scotland's modern minstrel.

"There, amidst the dust of the powerful de Morvilles and many a holy abbot and monk of old, and surrounded by the ashes of his own 'rough clan,' under walls scorched in many a Border foray, in the heart of the valley he loved so well, and of the scenes he sung, lie the mortal remains of that mighty master who has thrown a charm over the country, its history, and its traditions that will live as long as themselves."†

Jedburgh, with its beautifully interlaced arcade and Norman west door, belongs to the time of David I., and is a contemporary of Dryburgh; but being less renowned it suffered less, and in the sixteenth century became a temporal lordship of the Kerrs of Ferniehurst, ancestors of the present Lord Lothian.

---

* Autobiography of 1808. Lockhart's Life, vol. i., p. 66.

† I could not but quote these eloquent words of Mr Spottiswoode in the preface to the "Liber de Dryburgh," written in 1847. One's own words could not have done equal justice.

Melrose, fair Melrose, not the Melrose of the Lindisfarne monks, but that which David I. rebuilt, and Robert Bruce restored, intending "his heart to be buried there," is no more than a ruin, though the Duke of Buccleuch must feel, in his careful custody of this valuable possession, that no abbey in Scotland has more thoroughly done its work of connecting the past with the present.

St Cuthbert, who probably watched his sheep on the very spot where the ruin stands, near the monastery which Aidan had caused to be roughly built nearer the river, however legendary a character in the miracles with which his name is always associated whenever mentioned by our oldest chroniclers, has certainly the rare merit of deserving the thanks of centuries. But for him many records of the deepest interest, many buildings of the greatest value, would never have come down to us. To preserve his memory, and not only his acts and sayings, from oblivion, but also the supernatural influence which his name was believed to exercise, trained a school of men to that peculiar diary of events for which we are so grateful now.

Reginald of Durham, Symeon of Durham, the Venerable Bede, are instances of this; and their example was afterwards taken up in the Chronicles of Melrose and of Lanercost. The Chronicles of Melrose extend from A.D. 731 to A.D. 1264, and in the innumerable archives of this place historians can never sufficiently thank the industrious monks for the knowledge of history, of law, of customs, of institutions, which their charters, their seals, and their writs afford them.

Coldingham Priory, the first abbot of which was Herbert, in 1151, appears to have been in English hands under the bishopric of Durham till the year 1485, when it was attached to the Royal Chapel of Stirling; but long before then the Homes had looked upon the monastery as their own property, " setting the Pope and the Church of Durham at defiance," and when James III. appropriated its revenues they began that rebellion which cost him his life.

. But we have digressed sufficiently, and to Norham Castle we must return.

CHAPTER V.

PUDSEY.

1153—1176.

> " Never name in story
> Was greater than that which ye shall have won.
> Conquerors have conquered their foes alone,
> Whose revenge, pride, and power they have overthrown ;
> Ride ye more victorious over your own."—*Shelley.*

IN 1135 King Henry died. He never recovered the loss of his beloved William in the wreck of the " White Skiff." He never smiled from the hour that, on hearing the news which deprived him of all he loved and of an heir in whom he had placed all his hopes, he had fallen unconscious to the ground.

His nephew William, son of his brother Robert, was his heir, but Henry hated him.

His niece Maud, widow of the Emperor Henry the Fifth of Germany, was a favourite, and despite the seeming strangeness of seeing a woman succeed, Henry recognized her as his heir, and married her to the Count of Anjou.

On the other hand, Stephen, son of the Conqueror's sister Adela, married to the Count de Blois, was also a claimant to the throne, on the demise of his cousin William, which happened the same year as King Henry's death.

Brought up in England, his good humour and generosity had made him popular in London, the citizens of which, whose voice "had long been accepted as representative of the popular assent in the election of a king," poured out to meet him, on his approach to their city after the king's demise, with uproarious welcome, and swore to defend the King Stephen with "money and blood."

Thus the claim of Maud was set aside, but Geoffrey of Anjou was not likely to allow this without a struggle.

The late king had recognized Maud as his heir;—his council, at his suggestion, had ratified the choice;—Stephen had an elder brother, and the people of London were not the people of England: so reasoned Geoffrey.

Here was ground for dispute, and no wonder that for twenty years England became the scene of anarchy and misrule.

Among those who warmly embraced the cause of Geoffrey Plantagenet was King David of Scotland, and as a matter of course, his first exhibition of sympathy with Mathilda and dislike for Stephen was practically evinced in the invasion of Northumberland, which he entered from Coldstream, laying siege to the castle of Wark, then belonging to Walter Espec under a grant of Henry I.

David and his son Henry invested the castle with battering rams and other machines, but with no

F

success, and the siege was raised after three weeks.

Gathering together all the soldiers of fortune he could meet with, "the infamous army" overran the whole county to the Tyne, and no one could tell their number, "for multitudes uncalled for allied themselves with these for the love of plunder and of revenge, or for the desire of mischief."

The land of St Cuthbert was reserved till their return. Accounts abound of the horrors committed and of the superstition exhibited. Thus while the Abbey of Newminster was destroyed, that of Hexham was spared, because it was dedicated to St Andrew, the patron Saint of Scotland.

Meanwhile Stephen advancing into Northumberland found the enemy dispersed. They had fled in all directions on his approach, but he marched on to the Scottish Border, and David secretly followed him to Roxburgh, where he laid a snare to the English king, who was only saved by a timely warning; but disgusted with his expedition against an invisible foe, he marched south again, whereupon David and his plunderers appeared before Norham, 1138.

At first the castle was defended with great vigour by nine knights and their followers. Attack upon attack was gallantly repulsed, and the castle on the rock was proving to be invaluable, when the number of the defenders being greatly diminished by those who were helplessly wounded, it was resolved to capitulate, although the "fortifications were uninjured, and the castle was abundantly provisioned."

The names of the nine knights do not appear, but Asketillus was the Constable first appointed by Flambard, and it is probable that he died of his wounds on the present occasion.

No date of his death is recorded, but as he and the garrison and the townsmen of Norham, as well as Bishop Galfrid Rufus, were much blamed for giving up such a fortress after so short a siege and allowing it to be thus undermanned, it is at once evident why the names of the knights have not been preserved.

David's progress was stayed on the 22d of September 1138, when the battle of the Standard won by Walter Espec and the old Archbishop of York, "Turstin," aided by Robert de Brus, Bernard de Balliol (Scotch peers as well as English landowners), William de Albemarle, Robert de Ferrars, and William de Percy, obliged the Scottish king to return in due haste.

Again he attacked Wark but with no success, but there being "only one live horse and one in salt" left as nourishment for the garrison, the fortress at last surrendered on the news of the victory of the Standard; and David in admiration for the prowess shown by the besieged allowed the garrison to march out with their arms and equipments, and even presented them with twenty-five horses to replace those they had slain for nourishment.

At this stage, Alberic, Bishop of Ostia, the Pope's Legate, actively interfered in favour of peace throughout England. In the north he settled the preliminaries of a peace which was concluded in 1139 between the Scotch and the English, one of the principal articles of which stipulated that David's son Henry should receive the Earldom of Northumberland at the hands of Stephen, but that "no interference should be attempted with the rights of the Bishop of Durham within the territory of St Cuthbert," and in accordance with this stipulation Norham was given back to the English.

But David by this time had likewise understood the importance of having a bishop at Durham friendly to his interests.

Having been baulked in his attempt to obtain a control of the bishopric by a transfer of the homage of Geoffrey Rufus, Flambard's successor, from Stephen to himself, he tried on the death of Geoffrey to have his chancellor, William Cumin, who had been made prisoner at the battle of the Standard, appointed bishop in his stead, but though he intrigued for several years, William de St Barbara was finally appointed by Stephen, and took possession of the see in 1144.

"Time and the hour run through the roughest day," and the year 1154 died with promises of peace, such as England had not enjoyed for a quarter of a century.

David died early in the year, leaving a grandson Malcolm to inherit his crown, and another (William) that of the Earldom of Northumberland.

In October Stephen died, his eldest son having predeceased him by a few weeks; the claims of Henry Plantagenet, the son of the Empress Maud, were recognised, and he was proclaimed King of England under the title of Henry II.

"Those who had opposed King Stephen now submitted. An edict was promulgated for the suppression of outrages, the prevention of plunder, the dismissal of foreign mercenaries, and the destruction of the fortresses which since the death of King Henry I. every one had built on his lands. Justice and peace were thus established throughout the kingdom."

In the third year of his reign, A.D. 1157, Henry obtained possession, by negotiation with Malcolm, of Northumberland and Cumberland, and at once proceeded to fortify Bamborough, Newcastle, and Wark, while he gave instructions to Bishop Pudsey to repair Norham.

The bishop who must now engage our attention was a nephew of King Stephen, and therefore a privileged being.

Born in 1128, Hugh de Pudsey gave hopes from his illustrious birth that at an early age he would adorn by his personal merits any high position which he might attain, but such hopes are often illusory, and from a manuscript of the time we gather that "his countenance and character were affected," that he was "a great dissembler," and that "his specious virtues and professions of honour were hypocritical and delusive."

The charge is not very well sustained, however, though in the temper of the times, his innate vanity and natural ambition combined, which made him exercise a patience and moderation for which his subordinates were not prepared, may well have impressed them with the notion that he was not what he seemed to be.

Before he was twenty-five years of age he was Treasurer of York and Archdeacon of Winchester. When he had reached the age of twenty-five he was elected to the See of Durham with the king's concurrence, but against the will of Henry Murdac, Abbot of Clarevalle, and a pupil of St Bernard.

Much squabbling ensued, and a journey to Rome, "which attracted the attention of all the people upon the reverend troop."

Hugh came back absolved from the minor excommunication launched against him by the fiery Abbot of Clarevalle, and was consecrated in Rome.

On the 2nd of May 1154 he was enthroned at Durham, and from that time he applied himself to works of utility, which do him the greatest credit even to this day.

Besides endowing many a monastery with lands for their maintenance, and embellishing churches with ornaments of gold, silver, precious stones, he brought over from the continent marbles of various kinds with a view of adding to the magnificence of his cathedral church. Struck by the strange exclusion of women from the neighbourhood of the shrine of St Cuthbert, he constructed the beautiful gallilee at the west end for their reception; and by the advice of his uncle, and through the medium of his architect Richard, whose ability had earned for him the expressive cognomen of the "Ingenious,"* and who, a citizen of Durham, was renowned all over the country, he completed the fortress of Norham, which David had so wantonly damaged two years after its surrender, out of spite to Bishop Galfrid, because he did not renounce his allegiance to Stephen in favour of the Empress Maud.

The castles of the Anglo-Norman kings and barons, which were generally on an eminence and near a river, usually occupied a site of great extent and of irregular figure. They were surrounded by a broad ditch or *fosse*, sometimes filled with water and sometimes dry. Before the great gate was an outwork called a *barbacan*, which was a strong wall surmounted with turrets, designed for the defence of the gate and

---

* Vir iste Ricardus Ingeniator dictus cognominatus est, qui Dunelmensis civis effectus, cunctis regionis hujus incolis arte et nomine notissimus est.—" Reginald of Durham," ch. xiv. p. 112.

drawbridge. On the inside of the ditch stood the wall of the castle, about 8 or 10 feet thick, and between 20 and 30 feet high, with a parapet and a kind of embrasures, called crennels, on the top. On this wall, at proper distances, were built square towers of two or three stories high, which served for lodging some of the principal officers, and on the inside were erected lodgings for the servants or retainers, granaries, storehouses, and other necessary offices. On the top of this wall and on the flat roofs of these buildings stood the defenders of the castle when it was besieged, who thence discharged arrows, darts, and stones on the besiegers. The great gate of the castle stood in the course of this wall, and was strongly fortified with a tower on each side, with rooms over the passage, which was closed with thick folding doors of oak often plated with iron, and with an iron portcullis or grate let down from above.

Within this outer wall was a large open space or court, called the "*ballium*," in which stood commonly a chapel. On the inside of this ballium was another ditch, wall, gate, and towers, enclosing the inner ballium or court, within which the chief tower or keep was built. This was a large square fabric four or five stories in height, having small windows in prodigiously thick walls, which rendered the apartments within it dark and gloomy. This great tower was the residence of the constable or governor.

Underground were dismal dark vaults for the confinement of prisoners, and sometimes the dungeon. In this building also was the great hall in which hospitality was dispensed, and at one end of which a place called the dais was raised a little above the floor for the highest people of rank to dine.

This account can be accepted as a very fair description of almost every castle in the time of which we are writing. Hartlepool and Norham were nearly twin sisters in this respect, and both were built on the above-named principles.

As we have seen, Bishop Flambard's structure had been no more than a keep or tower guarded by the natural defences of the site on which it was built, and surrounded by an outer bailey or ballium, for affording shelter to the inhabitants and cattle in case of siege, the whole being protected by lines of circumvallation on the east, south, and west, the steep bank of the Tweed affording ample security on the north.

When Robert Ingeniator visited Norham in 1154, he found that the keep required repair and greater height, that a watch tower was necessary to the west, that an inner bailey would add strength to the defence, while the outer bailey would best be sheltered by the addition of a barbacan. He raised the walls, converted the ridge roof of the second story into a at covering, and added two more floors.

Many changes were made at subsequent periods, " when a well stair was inserted in the centre of the west wall near the chapel, so as to provide a new and convenient approach to each floor, and was carried to the end in a raised turret on the keep." This was probably the work of Anthony Bek; and when artillery was introduced against it, Sir George Bowes rebuilt the north bastion, but the accompanying view, which is reproduced from an engraving of 1680, gives a fair idea of the work of Bishop Pudsey.

The measurements of the castle, as carefully recorded by Mr J. G. Clark, show that the space covered by the walls was 2680 square yards. The north and east sides of the keep formed part of the common curtain of the whole, while in front of the other two sides is a broad and deep ditch extending from the eastern ravine to the northern steep, and is contained wholly within the outer ward.

The curtain wall surrounding the whole was high and strong when it belonged to the inner ward, and unequal when to the outer ward. The walls range from 12 to 15 feet thick, and appear to be 8 to 10 feet at the summit, which at present is inaccessible.

In a footnote * will be found the details of measure-

---

* The plan of the castle is irregular, following the general outline of ground. Like Barnard Castle, its form is a sort of quadrant, the north and east faces 143 yards and 108 yards long,

The South East View of **NORHAM CASTLE**, in the County of Northumberland
From a print of the ruin in 1680.

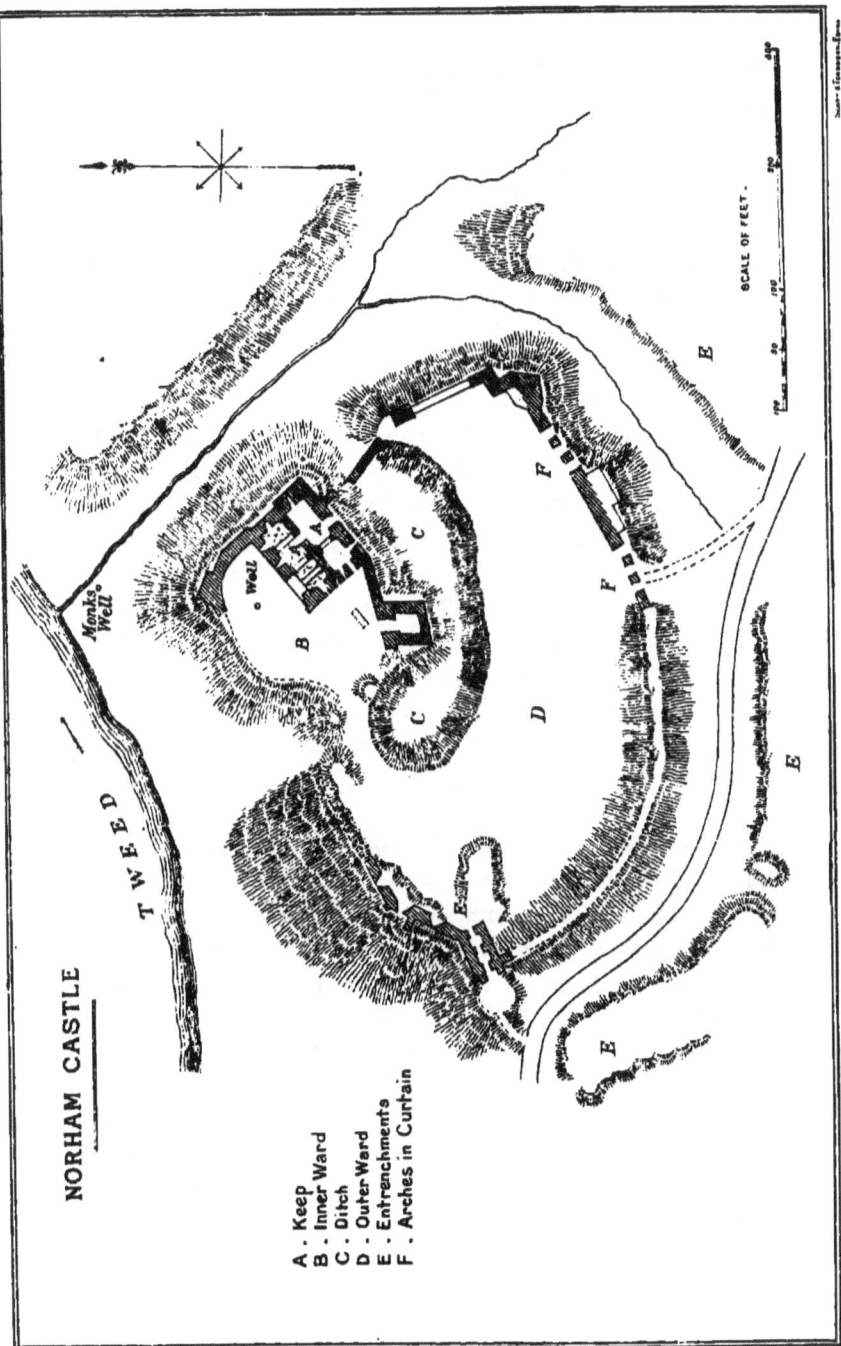

ment given by Mr Clark, as they will interest many, and are well worthy of preservation; and with his kind permission, and that of the Royal Archæological Institute of Great Britain, I reproduce a plan of the

being nearly at right angles and more or less straight, the border to the south-west, a curve of 223 yards, connecting the two sides. Of the area thus enclosed, the north-eastern portion is occupied by the upper or inner ward, the plan of which is roughly square, 57 yards east and west by 47 yards north and south, covering therefore within its walls 2680 square yards. The north and east sides of this ward form part of the common curtain of the whole. In front of the other two sides is a broad and deep ditch, which extends from the eastern ravine to the northern steep, and is contained wholly within the outer ward, the available area of which is thus considerably reduced. The whole was contained within a curtain wall, which when it belonged to the inner ward was high and strong, but when to the outer ward was unequal, being high where it crossed the beds of the inner ditch and along a part of the north front, but elsewhere either being low or of but moderate thickness. Most of the care of the engineer was lavished upon the inner ward.

The keep, the great, and though a mere ruin the best, preserved feature of the fortress, is rectangular, and measures at its base about 64 feet north and south, by 86 feet east and west, and is or has been about 90 feet high. The walls range from 12 feet to 15 feet thick, and appear to be 8 feet to 18 feet at the summit, which is inaccessible. The east end is a part of the exterior line of defence, and ranges with the curtain. The south face looks into the outer, and the other faces into the inner ward. The exterior faces have certain peculiarities. The south-east angle is capped by two pilasters, 11 feet broad and of slight projection, which, like the similar pilaster at Kenilworth, rise from a rough, bold, sloping plinth, 12 feet high, continued all along the east end. The pilasters have various sets-off, reducing them to 10 feet at the summit. They meet at and cover the angle, which is solid.

ruins and the ground which the castle covered. A section of the keep would be useless, as it was both heightened and lowered to suit circumstances.

Near the centre of the east end is another somewhat similar pilaster, only 10 feet broad, and beyond this the wall has been pulled down to the first floor. The part left forming the north-east angle of the keep had no pilaster, but is bounded with the northern curtain, which is of its age. The southern curtain is not in the line of the keep, but sprung from its south face about 25 feet west of the south angle, where it is seen to have been 7 feet thick and of the height of the first floor of the keep, or about 30 feet. This also was of the age of the keep.

The southern face of the keep, so far at least as its outer face is concerned, is of two dates. In the centre, but belonging to the eastern or older part, is a pilaster 8 feet broad, but without sets-off. Between this and the south-east angle above the curtain, and also without set-off, is another pilaster only 3 feet wide. A flat wall without pilasters, but with two sets-off near the summit, occupies the next 36 feet westward.

The base seems old, but the upper part is certainly later, though the decorated windows are probably insertions. Near the west end, about 6 inches projection, which ascends to the second floor level, and stops at the cill of a small-pointed doorway in the second floor, above this, in the two upper stories, are two similar but rather smaller doors. It is probable that these opened from mural lobbies in the gardrobes of timber projected from the wall; at least it is difficult to suggest any other reason for doorways so placed. The west face is all of one date, and, so far as the doors and windows go, of the decorated period. The wall itself is Norman. The curtain of the inner ward abuts upon the south-west angle, and is about 30 feet high and very thick, with a mural closet high up within it, which may be the gardrobe constructed in 1430-1. There are two pointed doors, both at the ground level, one leading into the south chamber of the keep, the other near the centre into a well stair, 10 foot diameter, which ascends

From these notes, and from all the information I have been able to gather on the subject, I have drawn up a sketch of what I conceive Norham Castle to

in the wall to the summit, and terminates in a raised square turret, a marked feature in every view of the keep. Six loops, one over the other, show the line of this staircase, and a few feet from the top and over the door are four or five corbels, which evidently supported some kind of bretasche of timber to protect the doorway below. Above are various windows, three of two lights, trefoiled square-headed, but decorated, and others of one light, but square labels. Towards the south end of this front, at the first floor level, is a large round-headed doorway, evidently the original main door of the keep, the outer stair leading to which is removed. No doubt this stair ascended from the north end, and the chamber in the curtain, now inaccessible, was either an oratory or a gardrobe opening from the vestibule before the door. This end, like the south, is tolerably perfect.

The north front is almost all removed. About 15 feet from the west end there remains one jamb of a door at the ground level. Beyond this, about 26 feet, is level with the ground. The remainder, about 40 feet, remains to the level of the first floor, and is pierced by two loops from the basement. The interior of the keep shows it to have contained a basement and four floors, the whole divided east and west, or longitudinally from bottom to top, by a party wall 5 feet thick, of which only the lower part remains. The basement at the ground level is composed of a north and south chamber, each 60 feet long, the northern 20 feet and the southern 15 feet broad. The southern was divided by a cross wall into two chambers, both barrel-vaulted, the western rather the longer. The eastern has a loop to the east, high up, set in a splayed rounded-headed recess, and in the north wall is a door leading into the north chamber. In the south wall, here 12 feet thick, is a breach 8 feet wide at the ground level, which probably represents a loop. The western chamber has a loop in the south wall, the recess of which runs into the barrel, producing a have been in its palmy days, when it issued in 1170 from the hands of Richard Ingeniator. · (The sketch has been perfected by Gray, Edinburgh.)

From the Norham gate the ground declines to the groin. In the west end is a doorway and passage through the wall, here 15 feet thick, and by its side a loop. There must have been a door between these southern chambers in the cross wall. The northern chamber seems to have been one room only, broken into four compartments by groined vaulting, between each bay being a broad flat band. There is a loop at the east end, and two others near it in the north wall. The two western bays are broken down. In the west wall is a loop, and near it in the north wall the jamb of a door of entrance, probably the stone doorway into the dungeon vault made in 1429-30, and fitted with an iron grate. This basement vaulting is about 10 feet high to the springing, and is original as at Bamborough, Mitford, and Newcastle, and the walls and loops all round, seen from within, seem also original, and their interior face work is excellent upon jointed ashlar. The remains of the cross wall show the first floor to have contained two chambers, both probably vaulted, the southern certainly so. Each was entered by a door from the western staircase. The north and much of the east wall of the north chamber is gone. In the west end is a decorated window in a large round-headed recess, flat-sided, and near it the entrance from the staircase.

In the east end was a loop in a splayed recess. The southern chamber was probably a lower and lesser hall. In the east end is a door from the well stair, and another door, large and round-headed, once the main entrance. Against the south wall are seen the remains of the vault of four compartments, groined, the bays divided by cross arches springing from the corbels. In the most western bay was a fireplace, in each of the three eastern a round-headed window in a splayed recess. In the east end is a pointed recess and a large lancet window, the whole evidently an insertion. The height of this floor was about 12 feet to the spring of the vault. The second was the floor of state, and in the original keep also the uppermost floor. The two rooms had low-pilched ditch or ravine which encircles the inner ward, and across this ditch in times of peace a drawbridge was lowered, which levelled the road from the entrance to the drawbridge to that of the castle itself.

open roofs, of which the weather mouldings are seen, as at Porchester in the end walls. These rooms are entered, each by its own door, from the wall stair, but the northern door has been built up and a loop placed in it.

Of the north chamber there only remains a large window in the west wall, in a drop arch or decorated insertion. If there was any fireplace it must have been in the dividing wall. The south chamber was evidently the great wall. In the east end is a large full centered Norman recess, containing a Norman window. In the west wall, besides the staircase door here pointed below a square label, is a pointed recess and window.

In the south wall are two bold round-headed recesses splayed to small lanced windows, and west of these a pointed door, probably entering a mural chamber, and communicating with the door already mentioned in the outer face of the wall. Originally there was no third floor, and to provide this the hall roof was removed, and for it substituted a flat ceiling supported by nine joists, the holes of which remain. On these were laid the planks of the third floor. Of this the north chamber had in its west end a segmented arched window recess, and a staircase door now blocked up. In the north chamber, west end, was a similar staircase door, and a pointed window recess. The east wall was not pierced, neither was the south wall, save by one window, and near it a small pointed door near the west end. The covering of this story was composed also of nine joists, which carried the planks of the fourth floor. Of this floor the remains are but slight. It also was composed of two chambers. Of the north, the west wall remains, but it contains neither window nor staircase door. The south chamber has in its west end a window, and in its south wall a fireplace. Of this wall only about 4 feet to 6 feet of its upper part is gone.

In war time, the drawbridge was up, and the outer bailey was deserted. Man and cattle were pressed within the inner ward, and only a detachment was left to defend the barbacan.

Within the inner ward was the chapel, which adjoined the hall and the kitchen, all against the north curtain; and according to a survey of the castle made in 1551, the chapel appears to have been " 30 feet by 18 feet, with walls 8 feet thick, and with a crypt below capable of stabling twenty horses, and a 'closet' above."

The well was near the north-east corner of the ward, and marks the general position of the kitchen.

The expenses of building were considerable; and from documents of the time and of a subsequent date, we gather that the making of a wheel for the well cost 33s. 4d.; that 2000 nails bought at Newcastle cost 26s. 8d.; that a plumber who "repaired the hall, the great chamber, and all the chambers, the kitchen and all the towers," received 33s. 4d.; that the carriage of a load of fuel was 12d.; that John Woodman, mason, received £26, 13s. 4d. for making the outer bridge of Norham; that "repairing the walls of the whole castle save the great tower" cost £8; that the salary of the constable was £50 for "guarding the Castle of Norham;" that watchers within the castle were paid 2d. a night; that mowing a meadow of 20 acres cost 10d. an acre; that the forester got 1d. a day; and finally, that the chaplain within the castle received 20s. a year.

It is true that the latter had not much to do at Norham, and was seldom there, evidently preferring to reside at Durham, for we find by some lines written a century later that—

> "And though a Bishop built this fort,
> Few holy brethren here resort.
> Even our good chaplain, as I ween,
> Since our last siege I have not seen;
> The mass he might not sing or say
> Upon one stinted meal a day,
> So safe he sat in Durham's aisle,
> And prayed for our success the while."

The smith who worked two iron doors at Auckland got £6, 13s. 4d. per annum over and above his dinner. Labourers got 4d., 4½d., and 5d. a day.

Walter de Scremerstone, a mason, received 3s. 4d. a week. John Nicholson, who carried 500 stones in carts, was entitled to 16s. 8d., while William Brady, who carried 60 stones in a boat, got 12d. only, or exactly half. Sixty chaldrons of lime were bought for £5; and a boat built at Berwick, which was charged £9, 18s. 7d., was found too expensive, and the sum was disallowed.

Bishop Pudsey hit upon a plan for defraying the expenses of building this castle, which was both novel and lucrative. One wonders that Flambard rather than Pudsey should not have been the inventor of the scheme.

Among the traditions of the diocese many were the wonderful stories related about St Cuthbert and his miraculous interference in all matters which seemed either unjust or unattainable in the land of his patrimony. Thus the story was current how a boy had been imprisoned by Malcolm in Berwick Castle, in a cell which from its filth and horrid darkness was called a coal pit, how dismal was the den wherein he had been confined, how cruel the manner he had been chained, and how ingenious the tortures invented to punish the wretched captive. In the depth of his misery he appealed to St Cuthbert, who in spite of bolts, bars, and fetters, freed him from his prison, and brought him safely over the Tweed to Norham Church.

It was reported how the man himself had wondered at his deliverance, and especially at the rapid travelling by land and by water which he had experienced without feeling his fetters, and how these had been hung up in the church at Norham to testify to the miracle performed.

In such a place the relics of the saint himself would be much venerated. A view of anything that had ever belonged to him would be much prized and valued, and no one would grudge the alms that might be asked for the privilege of beholding a strip from the garment of the saint, whether from the one he actually wore, or from the winding-sheet which had been thrown over his dead remains.

Acting on this conviction, Bishop Pudsey allowed his architect to carry with him to Norham a fragment of the original winding-sheet of St Cuthbert, which he had obtained from a friendly monk, who was wont to carry it in a little book suspended by a string to his neck.

Richard secured the relic in a pocket-book with some drawings which he was wont to carry on his person, and started on his journey.

For some time all those who gave him aid were favoured with a view of the relic, but one day as Richard had occasion to go to Berwick he lost his pocket-book on the way. An "envious" French clerk in Richard's employ found the pocket-book with the fragment, and "was rejoiced at his good fortune."

Repairing to his friends who were warming themselves at a fire, he at once proceeded to throw the relic into the fire, but behold it was lifted up on the crest of the flames without being injured. Not believing his eyes the Frenchman poked the fragment more into the grate, but no efforts to burn it were of any avail, and the "relic stood up as white as snow, and as it were purified like gold from the blazing furnace."*

Filled with remorse he hastened to his master, to whom he restored the relic with tears in his eyes, and thus ends the story, so that even the

* "Reginald of Durham."

Castle of Norham has its legend, as well as the village and its church.

In 1171 the murder of Thomas à Becket, Archbishop of Canterbury, was the cause of many of Henry's most powerful barons revolting against him, as they believed him to be a party to the foul deed.

Pudsey alone among the bishops of the realm conceived that he should join the discontented barons, and not only did he permit the Scottish army to march through his territories without opposition, but invited his nephew, Hugh de Bar, to come over from Flanders with 40 knights and 500 soldiers of foot.

These landed at Hartlepool on the very day that William, who had succeeded his sickly brother Malcolm on the Scottish throne, was made a prisoner, and Henry II. had purged his guilt by a pilgrimage to Becket's tomb at Canterbury.

The bishop was now in difficulties. He hastened to the king at Northampton, and while making his submission, he surrendered to him the castles of Durham, of Northallerton, and of Norham.

Roger de Coniers was then installed Constable of Norham, 1174, and remained in charge three years, when he was succeeded by William de Neville, who commanded under the crown till the death of Pudsey, when the castle was restored to the bishopric by King Richard I. in 1195, and Henry de Ferlington was appointed constable under the bishopric.

This was in consequence of a stipulation made at the time of the surrender to the crown, that the fortresses given up should revert to the bishopric, either on the death of Bishop Pudsey, or (under certain conditions) on that of the king.

In 1189 Henry died, and Richard Cœur de Lion succeeded.

Bent on distant journeys and on raising money, he released William of Scotland, for the sum of 10,000 marks of silver, and freed his heirs with the kingdom of Scotland from all subjection to the crown of England, besides resigning Berwick to the Scotch.

He traded on the empty vanity of the Bishop of Durham by giving him a share in the regency of the kingdom for the sum of £11,000, or £31,000 of our money, and allowing him to add an earl's coronet and sword to the Durham episcopal coat of arms, well knowing all the while that Longchamp, the other regent, would never allow Pudsey a chance of even expressing an opinion in the affairs of the realm.

Mortified and crestfallen, the old bishop, whose beautiful galley and silver throne, and preparations for a crusade on a regal scale, had all been appropriated by the crown, and whose prospects of governing England had sadly dwindled into an imprisonment in the Tower of London the day he attempted to act as co-regent with his brother bishop, took to eating plentifully by way of forgetting care.

At Crake he "ate to excess at supper of rich and surfeiting viands," and being taken ill he moved on to Doncaster, where, his disease increasing, and unable to bear the motion of a horse, he returned to Hovedon by water.

The doctors told him of his danger, but the old man, who was then threescore years and ten, would not believe them.

The hermit of Finchale (an abbey he had founded) had told him he would die ten years after he had been struck blind. He still possessed his eyesight. How, then, could his end be so near?

The prophecy was directed to the ambition and pride of his later days, but like most of us, the bishop could not see his faults.

His pains increased; his will was made; and on the 3d of March 1194, Bishop Pudsey breathed his last.

CHAPTER VI

KING JOHN.

1199—1216.

"In Coron's bay many a galley light,
Through Coron's lattices the lamps are bright,
For Seyd the Pasha makes a feast to-night."—*Byron.*

IN 1199 Richard the Lion Heart died, and, according to his wish, his body was buried at the foot of his father's tomb at Fontevrault, in token of his grief at having given him so much trouble in life; his heart was deposited in Rouen, as a mark of his love for the Normans; and his bowels were sent to Poictiers, in proof of how contemptible he held the disloyalty which Poitou had ever shown him.

Arthur of Brittany was heir to the throne, being the eldest son of Richard's elder brother Geoffrey, Duke of Brittany.

In 1103 the young man was brutally murdered at Rouen, and, whether guilty or not, King John, who was capable of any foul deed, and whose name is only remembered because he showed temporary pluck against clerical dictation, created France by his reverses, and made England by his submission to the barons at Runnymede, expiated during a life of trouble the blood of his nephew, which had been so foully shed.

In Scotland William the Lion was still king; and though his exploits do not appear to have justified the appellation, he was the first to blazon the achievement of Scotland with a lion rampant *gules* on a shield *or*.

Remembering how he had been deprived in his youth of the Earldom of Northumberland, he never relinquished his claims; and as the lion rampant was the distinctive badge of Northumberland, no wonder he adopted it on his own arms.

At Durham, Bishop Philip de Pictaria or Poicteu was consecrated on the 16th June 1196, for the purpose, it would seem, of coining money for his friend Richard I., for he had brought men with him to coin money in a mint which had already been erected, and a charter of privilege from the king.

At Norham, Henry de Furlington governed as Constable of the Castle.

Part of the Bishop of Durham's duties as King's Sheriff in the Palatinate was to receive the King of Scotland on the frontier, to escort him through his territories, and during such time "to allow him a daily pension of money, and to provide him with wine, with candles, and with spices."

Shortly after John's coronation William the Lion

preferred his claim on Northumberland, and was invited to come in person to visit the king at Lincoln.

At Norham, therefore, early in the year 1200, a motley crowd of great knights and barons in full military array, of priests and abbots in the bishop's suite, and the innumerable attendants of all these, might have been seen awaiting with some anxiety for the advent of the great Scottish lord, who was about to visit at his summons the newly-crowned King of England.

Berwick Bridge had the year before been carried away by an inundation of the Tweed,* and the question was whether the Scotch King and suite would come by Carham, or by Norham, or by Wark, or not at all.

Within the castle a banquet was prepared in the great hall, the garrison was lined all along the approaches through outer and inner baileys; the towers were gay with bunting, and a watcher from the west turret on the top of the great keep having sounded his bugle in token of approach, Bishop Philip, with mitre and crozier, advanced to the outer entrance, followed by the king's commissioners— Roger Bigot, Earl of Norfolk; Henry de Bohun, Earl of Hereford; David, Earl of Huntingdon; Roger de Lacy, Constable of Chester; Eustace de Vescy;

* "Bycause the arches of it were to low."—Leland's "Collectanea," 5, 1, 39.

Robert de Ros, of Wark; and Robert Fitz Roger, Sheriff of Northumberland.

Some fear had existed that the king would not come, for twice he had refused to answer the summons of King John, and only sent ambassadors, who had on his behalf held very lofty language; but all apprehensions were now dispelled by the gay display of the Scotch standard, and the arrival at the castle gates of Roger, Bishop of St Andrews, and Hugh Malebise, who had previously acted as deputies; of Patrick, Earl of Dunbar; and finally of the king himself.

Although the history of dress at this time does not record the splendour and luxury of subsequent ages, still the taste for it was growing daily.

An account of Thomas à Becket's manner of travelling may give an idea of what his imitators in the reigns of Richard and John endeavoured to realize, so as to increase their importance and impress people with their power and wealth :—

" Upwards of two hundred horsemen were in his train, consisting of clergymen, with knights, esquires, and sons of noblemen attending upon him in a military capacity, and servants of several degrees. They were all equipped with arms and clothed with new and elegant garments, every one according to his rank. He had with him twenty-four changes of apparel. No kind of elegance was spared, such as furs of the most precious kinds, with palls and suits of tapestry to adorn the state bed and bed chamber. He also took with him dogs and birds of every species that was proper for the sports of monarchs or used by the wealthy. Eight carriages followed, constructed for swiftness, and each one was drawn by five large beautiful horses; to every horse was appointed a strong young man, clad in a new tunic, which was girded about his loins, and every carriage was followed by a post-horse with a guard; in these conveyances the plate, the jewels, the sacred vessels, the ornaments for the altar, and all the furniture belonging to the chancellor and his company were deposited."

If a chancellor could do these things, what could not a king? what would not a commissioner of the king? And here at Norham, on the occasion of the very first pageant its peaceful villagers had ever beheld, were a king, a bishop of Durham, a viceroy of the crown of England, a Scotch bishop (the first of the independent hierarchy of Scotland just obtained), the most powerful earl of Scotland, and six of the greatest nobles of England, whose names, already illustrious, were about in the persons of no less than five of them—namely, Roger Bigot, Henry de Bohun, Roger de Lacy, Eustace de Vescy, and Robert de Ros —to become household words in the homes of Britain by being appended to the great charter of our liberties in 1215.*

* Stubb's "Select Charters," p. 306, from Matthew Paris.

Patrick, fifth Earl of Dunbar, having married a daughter of William the Lion, was the progenitor of the Earls of Home by his daughter Ada, to whom he gave the lands of Home, and who, having married her cousin, had made him take the name of Home.

No wonder that people had flocked from all the country around to see the mighty personages who were then assembled in the great castle on the Tweed. No wonder that the meeting has found its way into history and been recorded. The people who constituted it were well worthy of remembrance, and we read of them now with perhaps as much pride and pleasure as their appearance then gave delight and created admiration.

In the great hall of the castle was spread a sumptuous collation or dinner, of which the exact bill of fare has not reached us, but as Leland gives several which were served on the occasion of the "inthronization" of the archbishops and bishops of England from this time to a later age, it may interest the reader to know that there were generally several tables—the principal table, at which sat only the highest guests and the donor of the banquet, the abbots' table, the knights' table, the barons' table, and the lesser table. To each table were appointed a "marshall," a "sewer," a "conveyor of service," an "almner," a "panter," and two "butlers," and sometimes two and more under butlers. At the principal table all these officers were gentlemen, excepting the under butlers, who were yeomen.

There usually were two courses, between which various representations and musical entertainments took place. In the first course were the following dishes, which the reader may puzzle over as best he pleases :—

1. Frumentie ryall and mammonie to potage.
2. Lung in foyle.
3. Cunger p in foyle.
4. Lampreys with galantine.
5. Pyke in latmer sauce.
6. Cunger, roasted.
7. Halibut, roasted.
8. Salmon in foyle, roasted.
9. Carp in sharp sauce.
10. Celes rost r.
11. Salmon, baked.
12. Custard, planted.
13. Leche, Florentine.
14. Fritter, dolphin.

Second Course.

1. Jolie Ipocras and prune drendge to pottage.
2. Sturgeon in foyle, with welkes.
3. Turbit.
4. Soles.
5. Breame in sharpe sauce.
6. Carps in armine.
7. Tenches, flourished.
8. Crevesses d d.
9. Camprons rost.
10. Roches, fryed.
11. Lampreys, baked.

12. Quince and drendge, baked.
13. Tart melior.
14. Leche, Florentine.
15. Fryttar, ammell.
16. Fryttor, Pome.
17. A subtiltie with three stages with towers embatteled.

On copying these bills of fare, however, I notice that they point to a purely fish dinner. I must therefore give the bill of fare of one given by Henry VII. in the third year of his reign, on the occasion of the coronation of Queen Elizabeth, his wife.*

FIRST COURSE.

1. A warner before the course.
2. Shelder of Brawne in armor.
3. Frumetye with veneson.
4. Bruet riche.
5. Hart powdered graunt chars.
6. Fesaunt intramde Royall.
7. Swan with Chawdron.
8. Capons of high goe.
9. Lampervey in galantine.
10. Crane with cretney.
11. Pik in latymer sauce.
12. Heronusew with his sique.
13. Carpe in foile.
14. Kid reversed.
15. Perch in jeloy depte.
16. Conys of high grece.
17. Moten roiall, richly garnished.
18. Valance, baked.
19. Custard royal.
20. Tarte Polyn.

* See Appendix.

21. Leyse damask.
22. Frutt synoper.
23. Frutt Formage.
24. A soleltie with writing of balads.

Second Course.

1. A warner before the course.
2. Joly ypocras.
3. Mamanes with lozenges of gold.
4. Pekok in Hakell.
5. Bittowre.
6. Fesaunte.
7. Browes.
8. Egrets in Beorwetye.
9. Cokks.
10. Partricche.
11. Sturgyn freshe fenell.
12. Plovers.
13. Rabett sowker.
14. Seyle in fenyn entierly served richely.
15. Red shanks.
16. Snytes.
17. Quayles.
18. Larks ingraylede.
19. Creves de endence.
20. Venesone in paste royal.
21. Quince, baked.
22. Marche payne royal.
23. A cold bake mete flourished.
24. Lethe ciprus.
25. Lethe rube.
26. Fruter angeo.
27. Fruter monniteyne.
28. Castells of jely in temple wise made.
29. A soleltie.

The wine was plentiful—" vino rubeo," " vino

claret," "vino albeo," "de Ossey," "de Reane," and "de Malvesey."

In the accounts of Norham there is the following entry:—"For taking up a butt of Malwesse that should have gone to Norram, and the carriage of it to New Castel, 2s.; for bringing off the Malwesse, 11d.; and for Wyll's costs to Norham when he came from my lord, 3s."

On the 22nd of November 1200, King John received the King of Scotland outside the city of Lincoln. William performed the usual act of homage with the accustomed reservation as regards the lands he held or claimed to hold in England, and then renewed his demand of the counties of Northumberland and Cumberland.

"After a long discussion no agreement could be come to, and the King of England demanded of the King of Scotland a truce till the following Whitsuntide to afford time for deliberation. This being agreed to, William returned home with the same escort which attended him to Lincoln, where he remained only a single night."

For eight years this truce was prolonged till the year 1209, when, in the month of April, King John and King William first met at Bedlington, near Newcastle, and afterwards at Norham, where the negotiations were extended from the 23d to the 26th, and again without any satisfactory result, the fact being that in all probability John, of whom the saying was that "foul as it is, hell itself is defiled by the fouler presence of John," had only come to Norham for the purpose of ascertaining its strength and that of the castle's, which he visited on his way thither, and thus better understand the means at his disposal, either to invade his friend's territory or defend himself against retaliation, and still more to find out the flaws in those castles which he was invited to, and which belonged to that powerful nobility of which he was so soon to learn the strength.

Both on his way to Norham and on his return King John visited Eustace de Vesci at Alnwick, Roger de Merley at Morpeth, Roger Bertram at Mitford, and Robert de Ros at Wark. He saw the new fort erected at Tweedmouth, opposite Berwick, by the bishop; and though he left Norham on the 27th of April, he was back at Tweedmouth on the 3d of August, with an army at his back, ready to invade the territory of William.

But a war requires a pretext, and this was not so easily found. It has to be looked for in the events which had taken place during the eight years' truce, and in the temper in which they had left the king.

The murder of Arthur had roused Poitou, Anjou, and Touraine in revolt, and Philip of France was welcomed everywhere as the deliverer from the assassin king. Even Normandy "settled down into the most loyal province of France," 1203; and on the surrender

H

of Chateau Gaillard, the "castle saucy" of Richard I., which was the key to Rouen, John, whose plans of defence had been conceived with military genius, had to resign himself to the loss of his French possessions, which were the hereditary lands of his forefathers.

"Quick to discern the difficulties of his position, and inexhaustible in the resources with which he met them," John endeavoured to raise a great league against Philip, which nearly succeeded, and jealously noted for future vengeance all those who harboured his enemies or gave them help against him.

His reverses in France were followed by more serious troubles in England.

Bent on reconquering his lost provinces in France, he assembled an army at Portsmouth in the summer of 1205; but the primate of England, Hubert Walter, and the Earl Mareschal, in the name of the nobles, protested, and the king had to give up his darling project.

A double rancour was now gnawing at his soul, and the barons of England were, next to Philip, the objects of his hatred.

The primate, too, was against him; this must not occur again.

Just as if he were likely to be served in this respect, Hubert Walter died almost immediately after the successful protest.

John de Grey, Bishop of Norwich, was elected

primate at the king's request, although a rival had already been chosen.

Both candidates appealed to Rome, and the result was that neither got the appointment; but Innocent III., selecting an English priest, then at Rome, to receive the Cardinal's hat, called Stephen Langton, sent him to England as Archbishop of Canterbury to "free the Church of England from the royal tyranny."

John's fury knew no bounds, and it must be allowed the step was, on the part of Innocent, an unjustifiable usurpation of the rights both of the British clergy and the British crown, notwithstanding that Langton proved himself subsequently to be one of the greatest and most patriotic of English prelates.

The clergy were not powerful barons, and John could use them as he pleased. He threatened to banish them from the country if Langton was not at once recalled.

Innocent maintained the appointment, and threatened first, then placed an interdict upon the land, 1208.

No worship of any kind was permitted. The churches were closed; the bells that called to services were dumb; the newly-born were not baptized; the marriage ceremonies were stopped; the dying were deprived of consolation, and the administration of communion ceased.

A gloom fell upon the whole country, disturbed

only by the retaliatory measures of the king, who confiscated lands belonging to the clergy, afforded them no protection whatever, and let loose upon their vast numbers the rabble and plundering element in the population.

It was in the midst of these conflicts with the pope, with his clergy, with his barons, and with France that the king marched north in April 1209, and having previously noted with his keen eye the spirit of Northumberland, resolved to overawe the north by his presence in the summer of the same year.

William had given refuge to many English nobles, knights, and hunted priests within his own dominion as they fled from an interdicted land governed by a revengeful monarch, and no wonder.

Not satisfied with Tweedmouth as a residence, John arrived at Norham on the 4th of August, and here negotiations were carried on.

John, says Wendover, "bitterly reproached William with having received into his kingdom his fugitive subjects and avowed enemies, and with aiding and encouraging them in their enterprises against him."

William, anxious not to lose his chance of pushing forward the claims he never forgot, argued as well as he could, and finally entered into an agreement by which he was to give John 12,000 marks of silver as a security for peace, and was to be allowed to pull down the castle opposite Berwick. This was the peace of Norham.

Thus Norham again came to the fore at a critical moment, and received in the first visit which a king of England had paid it, one of the craftiest, and undoubtedly not the least intelligent, of the sovereigns of this realm.

That John's armed advance to Berwick on this occasion was one more diplomatic than military is plain from the fact that a display of strength at that moment was necessary when the people were incensed against him as the author of their misfortunes. It was also necessary in a march throughout the length of England to ascertain how the ground lay, and who were for or against him. It was finally necessary to make an alliance with the King of Scotland, so as to prevent his invading England in pursuance of a claim which the king had no intention of granting.

That John managed these matters in a masterly manner is evident from the price which he obtained as compensation for an act which he knew William could not very well prevent without offending the laws of good neighbourhood and hospitality so strong in those days, and still more in the peaceful period which ensued until the death of William in 1214.

Secure in this quarter, he hurried from Norham to the south to continue his warfare with the Holy See.

In 1210 he was formally excommunicated, which in Catholic parlance meant that not only had he ceased to be a Christian, but, as an excommunicated king, he had no longer any claims on the obedience of his subjects.

In 1211, Philip of France headed a crusade against him, and in 1212 he was solemnly deposed, the Roman legate Pandulph proclaiming his deposition to his face at Northampton. Still John did not give way. He knew that the English nation was ripening into a patriotic race, to whom any foreign dictate from church or foreign power was odious and likely to be resented, and trading on this knowledge of the people of England, he gathered an army on Barnham Down, and sent his ships against Philip's forces opposite. The fleet destroyed all Philip's hopes, captured his ships, and burnt Dieppe.

Meanwhile the secret conspiracies of the barons in England were becoming more open; many knights were asking for foreign help against the "impious John."* Llewellyn of Wales and William the Lion's son Alexander, now King of Scotland, were corresponding with the pope, and at any moment a mine might explode that would crush the king for ever.

At this crisis he turned a political somersault; crouched to the pope, received Langton, and accepted his crown from Pandulph, in token of fealty to Rome; compensated the clergy, and endeavoured to conciliate the barons.

The effect of this was at once apparent, though its

* Impius Johannes.—"Chronicon de Lanercost."

"shameless hypocrisy" was only recognised later. It gave the king the means of invading France once more, and so successful was he at first that Philip for a moment seemed lost.

At this juncture a final battle, adverse to the English arms, though the English soldiers that fought in it were the last to give way, settled the question, and from the battle of Bouvines, 1214, King John returned to England.

Having given way to the pope, so as to prosecute his war in France, he was now to give way to the barons, so as to prosecute more leisurely his revenge for their disaffection.

At Runnymede, on the 15th of July 1215, he signed the Magna Charta, which was the embodiment of the laws of Edward the Confessor, confirmed by Henry I., for maintaining the privileges and liberties and rights of the people of England.

He had been compelled to sign, but he "nursed wrath in his heart."

Alexander of Scotland, prosecuting the claim which had been the bane of his father's existence, at the same time that he found willing help in the disaffected barons of the north, who had returned from London, where they had helped to compel the king to the act which we have just recorded, at once proceeded to attack Norham Castle on his way to Felton; but forty days of siege made no impression on Pudsey's walls; the castle was asserting its impregnable strength.

Thinly but manfully garrisoned, and well commanded by Robert de Clifford, the castle resisted all Alexander's efforts, who finally not to lose time left it in the rear and pushed on to Fenton, and thence to the siege of Bamborough, where Philip de Ulecote commanded, and which place likewise he had to leave behind him.

But at Felton, on the 22d of October 1215, he received the homage of the barons of Northumberland as earl of that county.

This act roused King John to the revenge for which his numerous late humiliations made him thirst, and supplied a plausible pretext.

On the 6th of January 1216 he appeared before Newcastle; then proceeding to those places which in the year 1209 he had so cunningly reconnoitred, he plundered and burned Mitford, January 7th; Morpeth, January 7th; Alnwick, January 9th; and Wark, January 11th,* all in the space of a week, from the 9th to the 16th of January.

Crossing the Tweed into Scotland, he burnt Roxburgh, January 16th, with all the neighbouring villages, laid waste all Lothian, burnt Dunbar and Haddington, January 18th, plundered the old monastery of Coldingham, and having taken the castle and town of Berwick, January 15th, he in-

* "Chronicon de Lanercost," p. 18.

flicted on its inhabitants every suffering which it was possible for Jew or Gentile to conceive,* having with him "a body of Jews to instruct his soldiers in the art of butchery,"† and lastly set fire with his own hands, "against the manner of kings,"‡ to the house where he had lodged and been hospitably entertained.

Alexander was unable to check so rapid and destructive a progress, and in retaliation advanced against Carlisle and Barnard Castle, the seat of Hugh de Baliol, where he lost the aid, counsel, and valiant arm of his brother-in-law, the great Eustace de Vesci, Lord of Alnwick, who was slain by a shot of a crossbowman of the garrison while reconnoitring the place.§ Unable to take possession of it, Alexander returned to Scotland, burning Carlisle and the abbey of Holmcoltram on the way back.

John rushed south, flushed with blood and success, to meet further difficulties, and find his rival, Philip's son Lewis, entering London, while he had to fall back on the Welsh marshes.

Here he contracted a fever, which he inflamed by a gluttonous debauch, and was just able to reach Newark alive.

* "Ubi cum rutariis suis feroci supra modum et inhumana usus est tyrannide."

† "Judeos secum adduxisse et magistros malitiæ illos effecisse efertur."

‡ "Contra morem regium."—"Lanercost," p. 18.

§ "Dun circuiret castrum equitando quærens infirmiora loca." —"Chronicon de Mailros," p. 19.

On the 17th of October he died, and his death was the signal for all the English barons to rally round the boy King Henry and the Earl Mareschal, and to desert the Frenchman, whom in an hour of need against a tyrant they had called to their help.

Lincoln saw the last hostile troops from France that ever trod the British soil in conquest, and Hubert de Burgh's victory at sea, when from the decks of his ships the bowmen of Philip d'Aubeny " poured their arrows into the crowded masses on board the transports; others hurled quicklime into their enemies' faces, and the quicker vessels with their armed prows crashed into the sides of the French ships," completed the defeat of the French, and brought about the treaty of Lambeth, by which Lewis promised to withdraw, and his English adherents were restored to their possessions.

Thus John's end brought with it that peace which England never enjoyed during his reign, and Norham under him rose to the rank of the first of English fortresses, while it remained the single bright spot to which he could look back.

From its walls John had obtained that respite which was vital to him in his hour of greatest need, and the stoutness of its resistance had given him time to come up with his forces, while it had proved to him that there were still a few in the rebellious north on whom he could rely.

CHAPTER VII.

EDWARD I.

> "It was in old times, when trees compos'd rhymes,
>   And flowers did with elegy flow;
> It was in a field that various did yield,
>   A rose and a thistle did grow.
> In a sunshiny day, the rose chanc'd to say,
>   'Friend thistle, I'll be with you plain;
> And if you would be but united to me,
>   You wo'ld ne'er be a thistle again.'
> Says the thistle, 'My spears shield mortals from fears,
>   Whilst thou dost unguarded remain;
> And I do suppose, though I were a rose,
>   I'd wish to turn thistle again.'"—*Old Jacobite Song.*

THE year 1290 had arrived. Edward I. was on the throne of England. Anthony Bek was Bishop of Durham, and ten candidates pressed their claims to the vacant throne of Scotland.

The years that had elapsed since our last notice of Norham had been years of settlement.

In 1219, Alexander of Scotland, Stephen de Segrave, procurator on behalf of England, and the legate of the pope, had met at Norham to settle various disputes, of which the number was legion.

In 1242 the old claims of Scotland over Northumberland were settled for ever, Tinedale remaining a fief of the Scottish crown, while certain manors in

Cumberland were reserved to the Scotch king in fief of the crown of England.

At the same time efforts were made to bring the law to bear upon the boundaries of the two kingdoms, and the commissioners of either country attempted the task, though the limits they defined were even then looked upon as consecrated by usage and constituting the ancient marches, and are those which even now divide the borders.

Northumberland had become incorporated into the English realm. Scotch claims were to have no more hearing, but English claims upon Scotland were now to arise, and to cause much bloodshed for several centuries.

In 1278 a note was sounded which showed the future temper of Scottish princes.

On the day of St Simeon and St Jude, Alexander III. did homage to Edward I., his brother-in-law, for his English territories in these words:—

"I become your man for the lands which I hold of you in the kingdom of England, for which I owe you homage, saving my kingdom."

"And saving to the King of England if he right have to your homage for your kingdom," said the Bishop of Norwich.

"To homage for my kingdom of Scotland," at once replied Alexander, "no one has any right but God, nor do I hold it of any but of God." *

* "Registrum de Dunfermelyn," sec. xiii., p. 321, page 217.

Misfortunes were about to pour upon the family of Alexander, and Edward, either in the interest of parties or in his own, was compelled by circumstances to style himself the arbiter of Scotland's destinies, and by arbitrating *de facto* in the case of the claimants to its throne, constituting himself in a manner the supreme lord of that state.

The exact title had perhaps no foundation in fact, but the union of England and Scotland, if impossible by matrimonial means, was too great a blessing not to sanction some diplomatic efforts for its obtention.

In the year 1285, Alexander III. had three children alive. By the year 1286, his daughter, the Queen of Norway, had died, leaving an only daughter Margaret. His eldest son had died, leaving no issue by a daughter of the Earl of Flanders, and the second son died without being married.

The queen herself died about this time, and Alexander was made to marry again in somewhat indecent haste, Juliet, a lady of great beauty and accomplishment, daughter of the Count de Dreux, in order to "reconstitute a family unto himself," 1285.

In the following spring the king himself had a fall from his horse, 12th March 1286, having chosen to ride in the dark along the coast of Fife opposite Edinburgh. He was pitched over one of the rocks near the present burgh of Kinghorn, and killed on the spot.

Within a month the Estates meeting at Scone appointed a regency in the absence of the Queen Margaret, now fifteen years old, in Norway, and messages were sent to King Eric and to King Edward,

While the former prepared to send his daughter, the latter conceived the notion of marrying her on her arrival in Scotland to his own son, by which means it was to be hoped that their descent would unite Scotland and England under one throne.

A dispensation from the pope was actually obtained, and the sanction of the Scotch Estates was given to the proposal, 12 bishops, 12 earls, 23 abbots, 11 priors, and 50 barons signing the act of consent.

As soon as Edward received these authorities, he instructed Anthony Bek, Bishop of Durham, to act as " the *locum tenens* of Queen Margaret in concert with the guardians of Scotland, viz., the Bishops of St Andrews and Glasgow, the Earls Comyn, Bruce, and with the advice of the Estates," and the bishop lost no time in repairing to Edinburgh.

But in October a rumour which soon spread, and which grew into a luckless certainty, reached the king and the alarmed people of both countries, that the youthful Queen Margaret had been lost in the Orkney Isles.

How she came by her death still remains a mystery, but ten years after it was supposed to have occurred, " a woman came from Leipzig to Norway, who proclaimed herself to be the daughter of Eric and the lost Queen of Scotland." She said she had been followed to Orkney and kidnapped and sold, and she gave circumstantiality to her tale by naming as the perpetrator a woman of high rank, Ingebjoerg, the wife of Thore Haakonsson.

King Haco, who had succeeded his brother Eric, had her tried as an impostor and sentenced to death by burning. The sentence was executed at Bergen, and on her way to the stake, the poor woman told how as a child she had been at that very port with her father King Eric when she sailed for Scotland. An expiatory chapel marks the spot where she was burned. The people believed what justice had condemned.

This last stroke of misfortune, while it laid Scotland open to civil war unless matters were promptly settled between the competitors for the throne, was of very great moment to Edward, who thenceforth saw that his only chance of sovereignty over that country lay in the assertion of his overlordship, and the homage to be required by all claimants in proof of such paramount power.

He was still to learn that the Scottish throne was only to be held, as the late king had said, "from no one but God."

As soon as King Edward heard of the death of the young queen he hurried north, but the death of his wife Eleanor, November 28, 1290, obliged him to delay his departure northwards, so that he only reached Darlington on the 15th of April 1291.

Here he issued summonses to fifty-seven of his military tenants in the north of England, enjoining them to meet him, and "accompany him with horse and arms, and all the service they owed him, at Norham for six weeks reckoning from Easter," then proceeded to Newcastle where he spent the Easter festivities. The munificence of his alms was such, that according to an old chronicle of the time, "many, attracted by the liberal donations, were not ashamed to appear poor, so as to partake of them." *

He then proceeded to Alnwick, which still belonged to the family of de Vescy or Vescy, but which was shortly to be made over to Bishop Bek, and sold by him to the Percys, and punctual to a day he arrived with his large retinue at Norham Castle on the 9th of May. If Norham had once before seen a pageant worthy of remembrance, all memory of it was to be eclipsed by the splendour of the present gathering; and while notice is being sent to the Scotch claimants to bring their case before the king on the 31st May, it may be interesting to note those personages who were gathered round the mighty Edward.

And first and foremost was Sir Roger Brabazon, accompanied by Master Henry de Newark and John, son of Arthur of Cadomo.

* "Multi, partitione tam larga allecti, non erubescerent pauperes se prætendere."—" Lanercost," p. 140.

These were the legal advisers of the crown, who were understood to be impartial, and to have no connection whatever with the parties interested.

John de Cadomo was the notary public who minuted the events as they occurred, and certified by his signature to their correctness. Against these minutes there was no appeal.

Chief-Justice Sir Roger Brabazon drafted the summonses to be sent out, and Master Henry, being in a way the king's private secretary, most carefully introduced into the royal state papers such phrases as embodied the king's wishes and commands. All these being men of the law were dressed very plainly— " a coat of mixed stuff girt about them, with a girdle of silk ornamented with small bars or stripes of different colours," and a white coif or close cap of silk.

Still their appearance must have been striking, for if the "coif" was white, the coat or gown was scarlet faced with blue, and the shoes were scarlet.

Then came the warrior Bishop of Durham, Anthony Bek, with a mitre "embellished with pearls like the head of a queen, and a staff of gold set with jewels as heavy as lead," clothed in double worsted to the heels, with broad buckler and long sword, riding on his courser like a knight with his horses and his hounds, and his hood ornamented with precious stones, and followed by abbots in gay gowns of scarlet and green ornamented with cutwork, and long pikes to their shoes; by monks with long sleeves to their tunics edged with fur, "their hood fastened beneath the chin with a golden pin, and bells on their horses' bridles, jingling as they rode;" and by friars whose appearance was "not that of a poor man in a threadbare cape, but more like the pope himself."

The king himself, arrayed in a gorgeous robe of scarlet silk, over which a tabard or mantle was thrown, covering the front and the back of the body, but open at the sides from the shoulders downwards, richly embroidered with the arms of France and England, a brooch of gold on his breast, and every kind of jewel on his shoulders, wearing a crown of gold on his head, was a sight to behold.

The courtiers were no less magnificently arrayed, and conspicuous among the host of office-bearers was one "with a cap of gay colours, with ass's ears and cock's-comb, a fool's sceptre, and bells attached to his cap and dress, with legs of a goat and the thighs of a sparrow," who, though but the court jester, had saved his king and master at the siege of Ptolemais.

The knights mostly rode in military array, and their dark coat of mail, breeches of mail, and hood of mail, which covered both head and neck, were only enlivened by the rich appearance of their saddles and harness, on which their coats of arms were embroidered, and by the gold spurs which marked their rank.

Behind them came the squires or knights companions, in short gowns painted green, with white and red flowers spotted all over; hose and shoes of white, locks curiously tressed, a blue cap, and a girdle with pendant ornaments.

Behind these were the squire yeomen, in coat and hood of green coloured cloth, upon their arm an ornamented bandage, and beneath their girdle a bundle of arrows plumed with peacocks' feathers.

When all this crowd of courtiers, prelates, lawyers, knights, and attendants on King Edward had found their way into the castle, which was then commanded by Walter de Roubiry, silence was ordered to hear the king's proclamation, which was read aloud in Norman-French by Chief-Justice Brabazon :—

"Touched by the condition of Scotland, deprived of her natural rulers by a succession of calamities, and involved in great perplexities, we are influenced by affectionate zeal for one and all of the community, who look to us for peace and protection. We have, therefore, asked you to assemble here, and we have come ourselves from distant parts to meet you, feeling that, as superior or overlord of the kingdom, it lies with us in virtue of such superiority to do justice to all, and to restore peace. We shall take nothing unjustly from any one, nor refuse, delay, or impede justice to any one; but as superior or overlord will do ample justice to each and all. Therefore, for the facilitation of business, and that we may have the benefit of their assistance in transacting it, all present shall do us the favour to acknowledge our right as superior or overlord."

Chief-Justice Brabazon then made this speech intelligible to all by showing the necessity of the king being recognized as superior of the kingdom, so as to insure impartiality in the arbitration; but things were not to be done in a hurry, and three weeks hence the Scotch answer had to be given—a proof of how desirous the king was to see matters fairly dealt with.

During the three weeks that elapsed the king visited the country. The village of Norham was in the height of its prosperity, the animation around was unprecedented, and various feuds occurred among the many knights who had flocked to the Tweed either to befriend their candidates or to attend on their sovereign.

William de Vesci had a natural son John, who resented his father giving to the Bishop of Durham the honour of Alnwick, and thereupon began to use very intemperate language.* The bishop, furious that a bastard should grumble at the gracious acts of a father (who was a candidate for the Scotch throne,

---

* "Tôt après cet hour William de Vescy donna l'honour de Alnewyk à Antoyn de Bek, euesque de Duresme, qui pur chaudes paroles de Johan fils bastard le dit William le vendy à Henri de Percy."—"Scala Chronica," fol. 197.

and appears to have given up Alnwick rather in a hurry, and perhaps also because he had no legitimate sons), retorted by calling to his side young Henry Percy, then the squire of the Earl of Arundel (whose daughter he afterwards married), and informing him that he would sell Alnwick to him if he pleased. Percy purchased it for £15,000, and became, at the death of John, William de Vescy's brother, in 1310, the first Percy, Lord of Alnwick.*

Among the other gentlemen who attended on the king on this occasion was Thomas Gray Hugtoun, son of Sir John Gray, knight and burgess of Berwick, and himself the undoubted author of the "Scala Chronica," whose son, Sir Thomas Grey de Heton, was soon to become Constable of Norham.

Thus, in the above two personages, we find that the ancestors of the two most illustrious families of Northumberland came into notice at Norham.

William Heron of Ford and his son came from the Till to do homage to their sovereign; and Sir Roger Heron, the son of William Heron, was the first to

* " The Baronage of Anwicke and the signorie
   Was first the Lord Vescy, but this fourth Henry Percie,
   Of Anthony Becke, Bishop of Durham, of noble memory,
   Did purchase it to him and to his heires lineally."

From the "Metrical Pedigree of the Percyes," among the Dodsworth MSS. in the Bodleian Library. Edited by D. A. Richardson, in "Reprints of Rare Tracts," vol. i., Biographical. Newcastle, 1845.

receive a coat of arms—three herons argent on a field gules. His male descendants died out in 1553, and his possessions of Ford, Twizell, and Tilmouth passed by marriage into the family of Carr, and thence, in 1640, into that of Sir Francis Blake, Knight, of Oxford.

On the 31st of May 1291, upon the little island opposite the castle, on a meadow upon which the new grass had spread its verdant carpet, and whereon the stately battlements of the castle groaned ominously, the king had a throne erected, and, surrounded by his counsellors, his bishops, and his court, gave orders that the claimants alone and their advisers should stand before him.

All around, from the castle downwards, a motley crowd of knights and squires and yeomen looked down with interest and fear.

The Scotch hills opposite were filled with equal crowds of expectant warriors, eager and intent upon the proceedings which were going to take place.

Here stood Florence, Count of Holland; Patrick de Dunbar, Earl of March; William de Ross, Baron of Wark; William de Vesci, Lord of Alnwick; Robert de Pinkeny, Nicholas de Soulis, Roger de Mandeville, Patrick Golightly, and Sir John de Hastings.

Then came (and his arrival caused commotion) Robert de Brus, followed by Comyn, Lord of

Badenoch; by ambassadors of Eric, King of Norway; and finally, by John de Baliol.

When these were all in their places the Prior of Bath and Wells, the famous Thomas de Wynton, got up and read the king's speech.

The king bemoaned the unhappy condition of Scotland, and came to its rescue in the hour of its need. The bishops, prelates, counts, magnates, and nobles of Scotland had been invited to bring forward reasons why the king's rights of superiority over Scotland should be impugned; but nothing to that effect was proffered, exhibited, or shown by them. It was true that the community had given some answer in writing, but nothing to the point, seeing that the objection turned only on the fact that the recognition of overlordship on this occasion did not prejudice the interests of Scotland. Thus the king, through his interpreter, ignored a third party existing in the councils of the nations—viz., the community—and accepted only the statements of the other two, of which the claimants formed a part.

As most of these held as much property in England as in Scotland—property which, as feudal vassals of the King of England, they knew had his powerful protection—no wonder that they all performed without a word of dissent the act of homage which was next required, and which ran thus:—

"Inasmuch as we have all come to do homage to

the noble prince, Sir Edward, King of England, we promise for ourselves and for our heirs, for as much as we can incur such liability, that we shall be loyal and loyally hold our kingdom against all who may live or die, and shall neither damage the king nor his heirs knowingly, nor disturb him if in our power. To which we oblige ourselves and our heirs by swearing on these holy gospels."

Each knight then advanced, and taking the gospels in his hand, kissed the book, and swore as follows :—

I shall be feudal and loyal and shall be true and loyal to the King of England, Edward, and his heirs, in life, in limbs, and in my lands, against the living and the dead.*

Those nearest in blood to the deceased king then put forward their claim.

Nicholas de Soulis was the son of Marjory, an illegitimate daughter of Alexander II. by Alan the

---

* "Pur ceo que nous fumes toutz venutz à la fay le noble Prince, sir Edward roy Dengleterre, nous promettons, pur nous et pur noz heires, sur quant que nous puyssons encure, que nous serrons leals et lealment tendrons de vous encountre tute gent qui purront viver et morir : et que nous les damages le roy, ne ses heires, ne saverons, que nous ne le desturberons a notre pouer. A ceo nous obligeons nous et noz heires, inter ceo sumes juretz sur seyntz evangels.

"Jeo serra feel et leal, et fay et lealte porteray, au roy Dengleterre Edward, et ses heires, de vie, de membre, et de terrien honur, encountre toutz qe purront viver et morir.—"Chronicon de Lanercost," fol. 1988.

Durward, and therefore a brother-in-law of the late king. But the Church of Rome, although it had already asserted the dogma in England that an illegitimate issue lost all rights to succession, had not proclaimed it as yet so emphatically in Scotland; it was, however, well known there, for this same De Soulis had, previously to these incidents, applied to Rome unsuccessfully to have his marriage with Marjory legitimized. Before the English prelates his plea found no response, and his claims in right of his wife were set aside.

For similar reasons the Earl of March, the Lord of Ros, William de Vesci, Roger de Mandeville, and Patrick Golightly, descendants of William the Lion's miscellaneous progeny, were not given any lengthy hearing.

Robert de Pinkeny claimed his descent from Henry, youngest son of Malcolm Caenmore, and father of William the Lion, who predeceased the latter. This claim was through the female line.

Florence, Count of Holland, was the grandson of Ada, sister of William the Lion; and this would have been a serious claim had there not been male descendants of William the Lion in legitimate issue.

David, Earl of Huntingdon, brother of William the Lion, had married Matilda, daughter of Ranulph, Earl of Chester, and his grand-daughter and heiress, Devergoil, had married John de Baliol, Lord of

Nivelles in Normandy, and of Harcourt and of Castle Barnard in England, besides inheriting the possessions and titles of his father, Allan, Lord of Galloway.

This lady, who had just founded the college which bears her name at Oxford, had two sons, the eldest of whom was now pleading for his great-great-uncle's throne. This was a serious claim.

The "Lady of Baliol" had a sister Marjory, married to John Comyn of Badenoch, who pleaded likewise on this occasion, but could not but plead second to Baliol; indeed it is probable that he only claimed for the purpose of registering the fact for future times and contingencies.

David, Earl of Huntingdon, had a second daughter married to Robert de Brus, Lord of Annandale in Scotland, and of Hert and Hertness in England, and her grandson, Robert, the seventh of his name since the Conquest, Earl of Carrick by right of his wife, was now a rival to his younger cousin Baliol.

It was at once clear that this claim also was directly contingent on Baliol failing of issue; but while acknowledging this fact, Bruce insisted that Alexander II., when childless, had had him recognised as his heir should he die without children.

This special title was dismissed on the ground that Alexander II. having had children since then, he could not dispose of the realm for his children, whatever he might have wished for himself.

It was true that Bruce was nearer by one generation than his competitor Baliol, and the question to be decided was whether the direct male descendant of the eldest daughter had prior claim to one who, though direct male descendant of the second daughter, was nearer to the throne in blood by one generation.

The point was debateable then, though it could not be so now; and in accordance with his desire to do justice to all parties, the heralds proclaimed the king's wish that the meeting should be adjourned till August 3d, when the parties interested met again in Norham Church,—not the old Norham Church of Bishop Egfrid, but a fine spacious church, built by Bishop Pudsey about the year 1160 as a sequel to the castle which, like the church, he had found in want of repair.

On the 3d of August King Edward informed the claimants that, as the competition lay between two candidates only, he had determined on prolonging the adjournment to the following year, when his good clerk, William of Kilkenny, Professor of Civil Law, assisted by forty men, chosen in equal numbers by Baliol and by Bruce, and twenty-four appointed by himself, should report to him for final decision the result of their deliberations.

With this announcement the king withdrew from the castle, and the many days of rejoicing in the little village were over. It remained, with its river, and its scenery, and its church, and its castle, expectant of what the future might bring, and proud that in its midst two candidates had arisen whose claims to the Scottish throne were soon to be decided in favour of one or the other.

It could not foresee that out of this gay meeting passions would become inflamed, and days were fast approaching when Scotland would be humbled in the bloody wars of the fourteenth century, and that the light of England was to be sadly dimmed at Bannockburn.

We do not follow the referees in their search for documents and their interminable arguments. Mr J. H. Burton, in his "History of Scotland," 1874, has exhausted the subject with admirable care and precision; but in the decision given at Berwick, in June 1292, in favour of Baliol, and in the act of homage which he at once made to the king in Norham Church, the seeds were sown which were to bring Wallace, and Brus, and Edward III. to the fore.

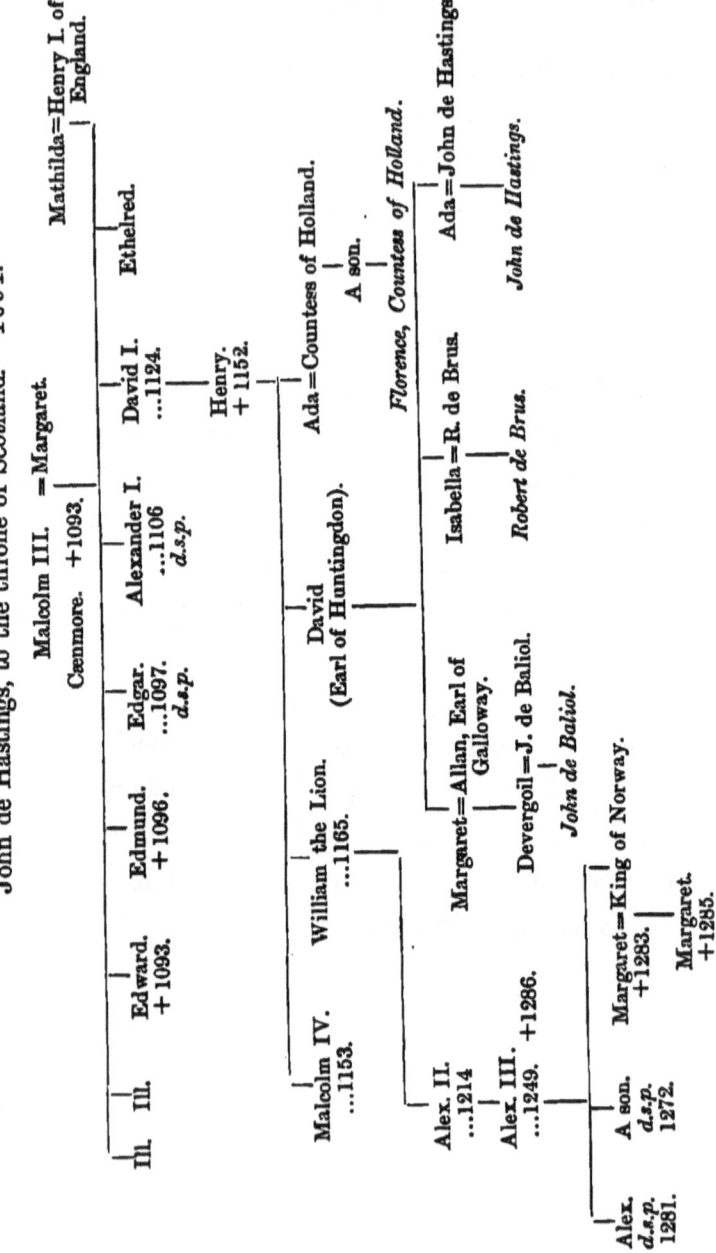

CHAPTER VIII.

WALLACE AND BRUCE.

"The star of the unconquered will,
  He rises in his breast,
  Serene, and resolute, and still,
  And calm and self-possessed."—*Longfellow.*

WHEN Baliol, as we have seen, swore fealty to Edward I. for his kingdom in the church of Norham, on the 20th of November 1292, there were those present who whispered to him that the kingdom of Scotland was not to be held from any mortal man, and who refused to submit to him or even to congratulate him much less to follow him to Scone for his coronation.

These were " the Bruces, father, son, and grandchild, together with John, Earl of Caithness, and William Douglas."*

Baliol was soon to discover that these men were but the courageous echo of the sentiments of the whole nation he was chosen to govern.

In Berwick he had been elected; from Berwick he was to receive the match which was to set Scotland and England at war for five-and-twenty years.

Roger Bartholomew, burgess of Berwick, "who

* "Martial Atchievements," by Abercromby, vol. i. p. 475.

owned a town in Scotland, had the unprecedented impudence to offer a complaint to King Edward against some of the officers appointed by King John of Scotland, that is, against the king himself. He was favourably heard, and justice was ordered to be done according to the laws and customs of England : than which 'twill be own'd that a greater affront could not be put upon the king and kingdom of Scotland."

No appeal from a Scotch court to that of his overlord had ever been allowed since the days of William the Lion, and the right of free justice was indisputable ; but Edward, in whose mind the original plan of obtaining the union of the two countries under one sovereign by marriage and lawful means had got lost in the maze of the discussions upon the overlordships appertaining *de jure*, as it were, to an arbiter, had forgotten that the *de jure* was only *pro tem.*, and had come to consider his rights as absolute and legitimate, and Baliol his creature, his viceroy.

Baliol, who cowed before the vigorous mind and will of Edward, wanted to give way, and came to Westminster for the purpose, but his people and his baronage forced him to resist.

Edward summoned him and the Scotch nobles to follow him in arms against the French. Baliol and the Scotch nobles refused, and allied themselves with the French against Edward. The Bishop of Durham was instructed to strengthen his fortresses, while, at his request, he was allowed to form part of the army which Edward ordered to advance on Berwick. Among the defendants of this place, which was so cruelly handled by Edward for having dared to taunt him—"Kynge Edward, waune thou havest Berwick pike thee: waun thou havest geten dike thee"—was a body of Flemish traders, who held the Redhall or town hall so stoutly under the command of Adam Flandrensis, that most of them were burned alive in it.

These Flemings had been banished from England by Henry II., and had settled on the borders. One of them, Berowald, had helped Malcolm IV. so materially in his struggles to put down the revolt of the Moray men, 1161, that he had obtained for himself and his descendants the lands and name of Innes. From him are descended the dukes of Roxburgh, and the present duke is the thirty-first descendant of Berowaldus.

The capture of Berwick was the easy prelude to an easier conquest of Scotland, the only fruit of which, however, appears to have been to secure a prison to Baliol instead of a throne, and a chair for the kings of England to sit upon at their coronation; for the sacred stone on which the old sovereigns of Scotland had been installed, and which legend asserted to have been the pillow of Jacob as angels ascended and descended upon him, "was removed from Scone, placed in Westminster by the shrine of the Confessor, and enclosed by Edward's order in a stately seat, which became from that hour the coronation chair of English kings."

But there was one on whom the misfortunes of Scotland had made a deep impression. He had just left the college of Dundee, and returned to his father's place at Craigie, when he heard that the King of England's justiciary, William Ormsby, was governing his native county with extreme insolence and oppression, and that throughout Scotland the English representatives were doing the same.

Gifted with a gigantic stature, he possessed enormous strength, and withal a pensive face, a poetical mind, and a will of iron. The most remarkable trait perhaps in his character, and which has made him so popular a hero, was the manner in which he brought his bodily gifts to be servants of his will, and that will in turn to become the instrument of his noble dreams.

He was the first to assert in Scotland what in England had been long asserted—that freedom is a national birthright.*

> * " Wallace, stature of greatness and height,
> Was judged thus by discretion of sight,
> That saw him both on Cheval and in Weed.
> Nine quarters large of height, he was indeed
> Third part that length, in shoulders broad was he,
> Right seemly strong and lusty for to see:
> In limmer great, with stalwart pace and sound,
> His brands hard, with armes long and round;
> His hands made right like to a palmeir

Who answers not to the cry of freedom? Launched at the head of the Scottish nation, even in this, one of their darkest hours, it found a noble response.

Outlawed and hunted like a wild beast in the caverns of Ayr, and near the Falls of the Clyde in Lanarkshire, Wallace eluded all pursuits, while he gathered friends and adherents wherever he went. Military service was not for gentlemen alone, said he. All men to arms who have a common cause to fight for: peasants and labourers, artisans and clerks, knights, barons, earls, and kings are one in a patriotic cause; and to this call there came in response a crowd of men who gave to feudalism its deathblow, and who constituted into a compact mass became the prototypes of those armies which Europe was eventually to raise at the expense of its working population.

> Of manlike make, with nails long and cleir.
> Proportioned fair and long was his visage,
> Right sad of speech and able of courage,
> Both breasted high with sturdy craig and great,
> His lippes round, his nose square and neit.
> Burning brown hair on brows and brees light,
> Cleir asper eyes like diamonds full bright.
> Under his chin, on his left side, was seene
> (By hurt) a wan, his colour was sangueene;
> Wounds he had in mony divers place,
> But fair and whole well keeped was his face.
> In time of peace, meek as a mind should be,
> When war approached, the right Hector was hee."

Old poem quoted by Hutchinson, "View of Northumberland," vol. ii. p. 57.

All answered to the call, and Stirling, 1297, saw the fall of the king's vice-regent, the Earl of Warrenne.

At last in 1298 the battle of Falkirk won by Edward stopped Wallace in his glorious career, and Scotland again was under English guardianship.

The hero pursued and betrayed fell into the hands of Edward, 1305, and, brought to Westminster, was tried and condemned on charges of treason, sacrilege, and robbery.

"Sir John Monteith, one of those he most trusted, brought a party of Englishmen upon him as he lurked somewhere near Glasgow, and carried him to London." *

His head was fixed on London Bridge, and his legs and arms were sent to Scotland and placed over as many cities of his native country.

> " Edward! . . . . . .
> But now the infamy is thine ;
> His end crowns him with glorious Bays,
> And stains the brightest of thy praise." †

Though ruined for a time, the cause of freedom was not extinguished. Though Wallace was dead, Scotland was roused into life. It was not for baron's

---

* "Martial Atchievements," book iii., vol. i. p. 543.

† ". . . . . sed scin quid in ista
Immanitate viceris ?
Ut vallæ in cunctas oras spargantur et horas
Laudes tuumque dedecus."
—"Martial Atchievements," vol. i. p. 548.

wish or king's fancy that Scotchmen now would have to fight. Wallace had pointed out the common cause; his words would never be forgotten.

A young man had noted the great mind which Wallace had possessed. He had claims himself upon the Scottish throne. His parents, though loyal to Edward as lords of Annandale in England, had never recognised the Baliol, and never praised him for his subserviency. "If he were only King of the Scots, the work of Wallace would be completed under his special charge."

He wrote in this strain to the Bishop of St Andrews. His letter was intercepted, and the boy flew to Scotland to punish the Lord of Badenoch, who had betrayed him, as he thought.

Before the high altar in the church of the Grey Friars at Dumfries, he reproached his cousin, and, regardless of the place, stabbed him in the heart, then rode to Scone, where the Countess of Buchan, sister to Duncan, Earl of Fife, placed the crown on his head, 27th March 1306.

"I fear we are only playing at royalty like children in their games," said Mary, his wife. "We shall see," replied Robert Bruce.

Indeed at first Mary's words seemed but too painfully true.

All went wrong: she was a prisoner, he a fugitive, and the Countess of Buchan exposed in a cage representing a crown in the streets of Berwick; but death came to his aid, and Edward died in 1307.

Bruce had then learned the value of adversity. Brave and genial in temper, Bruce had borne the hardships of his career with a courage and hopefulness which never failed him. The game of king and queen was not to be child's play. Light came little by little to illumine the darkness of his days and future. James Douglas rallied round him, thirsting for revenge, and to reconquer the lands of his father which had been given to Lord Clifford.

Thomas Randolph, Earl of Moray, came to his uncle's rescue, and a host of others.

Confidence revived in the sacred cause, and by the year 1314, although an army of near 100,000 men were marching against Bruce and his 30,000 adherents, so great had become his generalship, so hopeful his chances of success, so sanguine the Scottish expectations, that the battle of Bannockburn became not only possible, but the starting point of his greatness and his celebrity.

The battle has been rightly represented as the fight between the feudal and the free systems of warfare. On Wallace's plans the Scottish footmen had been drawn up in squares, on which the English cavalry broke, and could make no impression.

The day remained with the advocates of freedom, and the magnificent army of knights with their banners and brilliant horsemen were soon floundering in the pits which Bruce had caused to be dug to protect his admirably chosen battle-ground near Stirling.

Edward II. had lost Scotland in a day.

It was now the turn of the Scotch to pursue their victory over the Border, and Norham and Berwick were their first aim.

Old Bishop Bek had died in 1309, and been succeeded by Richard Kellow or Kellawe, who in 1311 appointed William de Ridell, Constable of Norham Castle, the same who was knighted three years afterwards on his reappointment to the same office.

This Sir William de Ridell, who received as a coat of arms a *fesse* between three garbs *azure* on a field *argent*, is the ancestor of the old Northumberland family of Ridell of Gateshead, Fenham, Swinburne Castle, and Felton, and they too had their beginning at the old castle.

On his way to Norham, William de Ridell stopped at Hagerdeston, where Edward II. had come to receive the homage of Thomas, Earl of Lancaster, for his Earldom of Lincoln, and was the guest of John de Haggerstone, the descendant of old Saxon settlers in Northumberland, of whom Raine says, "though their name seldom occurs in connection with the public history of the Borders, and are recorded by no monumental inscription in the parish church of Holy

Island, the burial place of the family, yet few families can boast such a pedigree or such a shield of arms." *

These Haggerstones have come down through time to the present baronet, and their seat was until very recent years the same old place whereon their Saxon forefathers had settled, four miles from Berwick and close to Goswick.

Lady Marjoribanks of Ladykirk, opposite Norham, is an aunt of the present Sir Carnaby.

Lancaster had been the prime mover in the destruction of Gaveston, and had incurred the king's displeasure, but the meeting at Haggerstone had brought about a temporary reconciliation.

He returned to Lincoln, where parliament met to grant supplies for prosecuting the war against the Scots, whose ravages in Northumberland and in the lands of the Palatinate had been such that "famine raged throughout these lands, that wheat sold at 40s. a quarter (which is nearly £5 of our own money), that children were hid with all imaginable care by their parents to prevent their being stolen and eaten by thieves, that prisoners in goals devoured one another, and that people died in such numbers daily that hardly could the living suffice to bury the dead."

Composition with the enemy became the rule, and if such composition constituted political treason, in

* Raine's " History of North Durham," page 224.

most cases it afforded relief, for matters were at their worst.

Bishop Kellawe in the interests of his suffering people had purchased a truce from Bruce; and the addled-brained King Edward II. ("there is always a fool between an illustrious father and grandson") could not be made to recognise the title of king which Bruce had fairly won at Bannockburn, and which would have put an end to his depredations, but suspecting the bishop of treason, he requested the loan of his castles of defence.

Walter de Goswike was appointed bailiff of the shire of Norham and keeper of the castle in the place of Sir William Ridell, and the following inventory of the armour and provisions shows that if famine was raging as violently all around as the account given above would seem to warrant, Sir William Ridell had taken care that the garrison of Norham should be well provisioned:*

>62 cod-fish (fresh).
>2200 stock-fish † (salt).
>18 cheeses.
>23 tuns of wine.
>6 carcases of salt beef.
>20   „   mutton.
>20 quarters of salt.
>50 pigs.
>3 goats.

* No salmon it will be observed.
† Stock-fish is still the German word for salted cod.

24 beeves.
34½ quarters of wheat.
52 ,, of barley in stack.
35 ,, ,, thrashed out.
7 ,, 3 bolls of barley in granary.
129 ,, of malt in the tower.
84 ,, of oats in the low hall.
40 ,, of sea coals.

The other articles were articles of war:

87 pair of leathers.
9 targets.
88 steel hats.
136 crossbows.
103 bandricks or belts.
9 pair of cuishes, armour for the thigh.
19 actons.
20 haubergeons.
154 pieces of iron.

And for domestic use there appears to have been:

8 table-cloths.
7 coarse table-cloths.
2 old towels.
8 tankards.
9 pots of pewter.
6 pots of brass.
9 pails of brass.
1 great vessel of brass for making candles.
3 caldrons.
2 basins.
2 wash basins.
1 wash basin hanging in the hall.

The furniture appears to have been scanty:

2 three-footed stools.*

* "History of North Durham," Raine, p. 285.

And in the chapel:

- 2 towels.
- 1 chalice, parcel gilt.
- 2 old missals, and a set of priest's vestments.

In 1316 Kellawe died, "moribus et vita dignus," and Lewis Beaumont was elected Bishop. On the 23rd of May 1316, however, Norham was restored to the bishopric, and the names of the commissioners who received the castle from the king are recorded as Walter de Gosewyk, who was continued in office, William de Brakenbury, Galfrid de Edenham, and Roger de Saxton.

Affairs in England had been going from bad to worse, and in Northumberland every place of importance had surrendered to the Scots excepting Alnwick, Berwick, Bamborough, and Norham.

An invasion even worse than that of the Scots was overrunning the unfortunate country. Robbers of every description were plundering whatever remained to be plundered, and their principal chiefs were Gilbert de Middleton, who was keeper of Mitford Castle, and Wallis de Selby, who had his castle near Wooler.

The pope had sent two cardinals, Gauselinus and Lucas, to settle matters if possible; but as they were not instructed to recognise Brus as king, their mission came to naught, and they returned to tell "how the Northumbrians, under Middleton and Selby, had robbed them of all they possessed excepting their clothes, and how the Scots had afterwards plundered them and sent them back naked to Berwick."

The Bishop of Durham, who had accompanied these legates of the pope some little way, was taken with them, and only liberated in the year 1318, on the 26th of March.

During his captivity, Sir Thomas Grey de Heton had been appointed Constable of Norham by the crown, and his first care was to put the place in such order as to hold out against any assault or surprise.

The Scots were becoming furious at the resistance which Berwick and Norham still made, and taunts of every description were levelled at the Governor of Norham. Northumberland was becoming fast the watchword of England as the place of danger, and Norham the most dangerous spot in Northumberland.

"About this tyme there was a greate feste made yn Lincolnshir, to which came many gentlemen and ladies."

The place in Lincolnshire was the Manor of Scrivelby, which was held by the family of Marmion, who having before the Conquest been royal champions to the Dukes of Normandy, had since continued to be the champions of the kings of England.

The direct line had become extinct in the person of Philip de Marmion, who died in 20th of Edward I. without direct male issue; but there were collaterals, and among others William Marmion, who married Lora,* a daughter of Richard, natural son of King John.

The Manor of Scrivelby itself had been confirmed to Sir John Dymoke, who was heir to it by one of the co-heiresses of Robert de Marmion, together with the office of champion—namely, of riding completely armed upon a barbed horse into Westminster Hall on the day of the coronation, and there to "challenge the combat against any who would gainsay the king's title."

At Sir John Dymoke's table sat, on a day in the year 1318, this William Marmion, the relic of an old family though a young man still. Among the ladies present there was one who had brought with her a helmet with a rich crest of gold, destined to William Marmion, knight, with a letter of commandment from her lady, the Lady Lora we have mentioned, "that he should go into the daungerest place in England, and there to let the heaulme be seene and known as famous."

Marmion at once got up, and accepting the challenge, bade the lady inform her mistress that to Norham forthwith he would proceed, and that he would there obey her wishes, and make the helmet known "as famous."

While on his way to Norham he fell in with the

* She afterwards married Richard de Berkeley, 1236.— "Collin's Peerage," Fitz Hardinge.

commissioners from England, who, eight in number, were on their way to Berwick to obtain a truce from the Scotch king.

But the embassy came to naught; for Bruce, who then was at Auld Cambus, twelve miles from Berwick, with his troops, had added to his resolve not to treat with the English until his royal title was acknowledged, that of not doing even this unless Berwick were in his hands.

The governor of this place was one Peter Spalding, a Scotchman by descent though in the English pay. The commander of the fort was Roger Horseley.

Spalding and Horseley were enemies; and in a fit of anger against his brother-in-law, Spalding sent a message to Douglas that if a party of Scots would, on a certain night, scale the wall at the Cowgate Port, which faces the Magdalen Fields, he would see that the watch kept on that night should not be strict.

The proposal was hailed with rapture by Bruce, who entrusted the expedition to the two heroes of Bannockburn, Randolph, Earl of Moray, and Douglas, the "flower of chivalry."

These met at Duns, ten miles from Berwick, and marched silently towards the town, opposite which they arrived about three in the morning. Going round by the Bell Tower and the Greenses, they arrived before the Magdalen Fields before any one was aware of their presence, excepting Spalding himself, who, anxious and desperate, was pacing alone along the Cowgate walls.

One by one the Scotch were admitted; and though it had been arranged that they were to remain hidden till the opportunity offered for a rush to the castle, such was the greed of Douglas' soldiery that before daybreak fighting had already begun.

At the Scots gate the Douglas with his battle-axe was fighting desperately against all comers, and Sir William Keith, who had just been knighted, was winning his spurs against the brave old governor, who came out of the encounter with the loss of one eye; but though hardly pressed and scarcely conscious, back to the castle he got with a few of his men, and the gates being closed, encouraged them to resist to the last, even though, as he knew, his last hour had come.

The castle "kept up for eleven weeks,"* and no succour arriving, surrendered at last; but Roger Horseley had died of his wounds long before.

The news of this surrender reached Norham just as a knight with a magnificent golden helmet was riding up to its gates and demanding admission of the governor, Sir Thomas Grey.

"I have come," said he, "to the daungerest place in England to let this heaulme be seen and known as famous for sake of God and the Lady Lora."

"You will soon have occasion to prove your

* Leland, vol. i. p. 547.

courage," said Grey, "for Berwick is taken, and the Scots will be here presently."

Indeed the "Scottes became so proude after they got Berwick that they nothing esteemed the Englishmen, and it were a wonderful processe to declare what mischief cam by hungre and asseges by the space of xi yeres in Northumberland."

As Grey had predicted, within four days of Marmion's coming "Sir Philip Moubray,* Guardian of Berwick, appeared before Norham, having in his band 140 men-at-arms, the very flower of men of the Scottish marshes.

"Thomas Grey seeing this, brought his garrison before the barriers of the castel," and looking round saw William Marmion on foot, "richly arrayed, as al glittering in gold, and wering the heaulme, his lady's present.

"Then said Thomas Gray, 'Sir Knight, ye be come hither to fame your helmet. Mount up on yon horse, and ride like a valiant man to yon even here at hand, and I forsake God if I rescue not thy body deade or alyve, or I myself will dye for it.'

"Whereupon Marmion took his courser and rode among the throng of the enemies; the which laid sore stripes on him, and pulled him at last out of his saddle to the ground.

"Then Thomas Gray, with all the whole garrison,

* Throughout history the Mowbrays appear to have been Scotch or English as suited their fancy, or may be their interest.

lette pryk yn among the Scottes, and so wondid them and their horses that they were overthrown; and Marmion, sore beaten, was horsid again, and with Gray persewid the Scottes in chase."

Fifty horses of price were taken, and these the women of Norham brought to "the foot men in the castle that they might follow the chase."

The brave knight Sir Thomas Gray "himself killed one Cryne, a Fleming, an admiral, and great robber on the se, and in high favour with Robert Bruce: the residue that escaped were chased to the nuns of Berwick."

A few days afterwards "Adam de Gordon, a baron of Scotland, came with 160 men to drive away the cattle pasturing at Norham;" but the young men of the country rose to the occasion, and fought desperately for their property.

Sir Thomas from the castle saw the fight, and seeing the Norham men unable to cope with such tried soldiers—"standing, in fact, in jeopardy"—sallied forth from the castle with only 60 men, and killed most part of the Scots and their horses."

Such daring deserved punishment, and Bruce sent a whole army to besiege the fortress.

For a whole year Sir Thomas was the butt of the attacks of that Scotch army, which had reaped so many laurels and was distinguished for so many valiant knights.

Two fortresses were raised against the castle—one at Upsettlington, a little below Ladykirk; and another at Norham Church, remains of which can still be traced in the churchyard a little to the east of the church.

Here every engine of war and besieging weapon was arrayed against the castle of "the fighting bischoppes." The balista, which shot large arrows; the catapult, which shot large stones, balls, and pieces of rock; the battering ram, for making breaches in the walls; the iron scaling-ladders; and the slings with which to arm (together with the bow) the soldiers on foot.

Here also were the fire instruments—the "armed dog" carrying a torch to set fire to a camp, and the "cat" with torch to set fire to a besieged place.

Inside the castle there were jugs in baked earth filled with quicklime to be thrown against the enemy, scatter their contents among them, "sprinkle them as with holy water, and enter into their mouths;" incendiary barrels to roll among the besiegers; chevaux de frise to spike the horses of the enemy; lances, knives, catapults, and slings.

With these and a trusty troop did Sir Thomas nobly hold out against his powerful foe. Twice, indeed, he was relieved by the timely arrival of Lord Henry Percy, second Lord of Alnwick, the same who was to receive the castle and manor of Warkworth for his distinguished services, and to take King David, son of Robert Bruce, a prisoner near Durham; and by Ranulph de Nevile, first Lord of Raby, married to Eufemia, daughter of Sir John de Clavering of Callaley, Axwell, and Berrington, in Northumberland, who was still Baron of Warkworth, and a direct descendant of one of the noblest families that the Norman Conquest had seated in the north of England.*

Meanwhile the besiegers went on with their work, and undermined a passage by which they had got in at dead of night into the outer bailey, their scaling efforts having proved utterly useless, their fire-engines powerless against the strong walls, their battering rams of no avail, and the ardour of the most zealous destructive to themselves.

They kept the outer bailey three days, but not an hour longer, and a brave onslaught of Grey and his small garrison put the Scotch to flight, and restored the old castle to its natural strength..

After a year's fruitless attempt the task appeared to be given up; but the Scotch returned with pertinacity, and a seven months' siege was no more successful than the first.

Unfortunately the resistance of Norham was of no

* The last of the Claverings of Callaley married, in 1859, Sir Henry Paston Bedingfeld of Oxburgh, and the old family seat was sold to Mr Brown in 1880.

avail, for Wark had fallen into the hands of the Scots, and they could thus leave Norham behind them, and ravage Northumberland and Durham at their leisure.

But while everything was giving way before the prowess of Bruce and his army, while castle, fortress, and camp were surrendering to his victorious banner, the stout old Border castle, the queen of Border fortresses, was reminding Bruce of the humiliations of his younger days, and teaching Edward how a brave Northumbrian knight could do his duty to his king if the king forgot to do his by his people.

In 1322, Edward, who "kept much the sea-coasts and delighted in ships, too much using the vile company of maryners, whereby he lost much favour of his people,"* heard that Norham was besieged again, and that he must come to its relief.

He, therefore, summoned all his military tenants at Newcastle for the express purpose of relieving Norham, not venturing on a second attempt to recover Berwick, in which he had so signally failed two years before (1319); but the rapidity of Bruce's movements obliged him to return with all speed to Yorkshire, where he was nearly made prisoner, and lost his privy seal for the second time. Edward II. seems to have attached much price to this seal, for again, as he had after Bannockburn, he issued a proclamation promising a reward for its recovery.

* Leland's "Collectanea," vol. ii. p. 549.

Norham, a third time under the valiant Grey, withstood the new engines and machines brought against it, 1322; but in 1326, Bruce himself came before its walls, resolved not to leave them until he had planted his standard upon the keep.

Robert Maners had succeeded the veteran Sir Thomas Grey, of whom it was said, "Many other great deeds and feats of arm did he accomplish which are not recorded," but whose name will ever remain with those of Flambard and Pudsey, one of the glories of which Norham Castle boasts.

Stoutly did Maners maintain the reputation of Norham for strength. Once he suffered sixteen assailants to scale the wall; but when they had got over it, they were put to the sword by a party of his men lying in ambush against the walls within, unseen and unsuspected of the besiegers.

In 1327, however, a similar ruse may have been again resorted to, and too great a rush of men have been allowed to scale the walls, for the castle was taken by storm, "three knights of great military fame in the Scotch army falling in the attack—William de Montraud, John de Clapham, and Maillis de Robery."

It was during this siege that "Thomas Grey, sone of the late governor, who had been three tymes besegid by the Scottes in Norham Castel in King Edwarde the Secunde dayes," sallied forth with fifty men of the garrison to engage "a bannaret with his banner and four hundred men," who had been sent to collect forage by Patrick, Earl of March, who was "imbuschid upon the Scottish side of Twede.

"Lighting apon foote, and not knowing of Patrick's band behynd, Grey set upon the foraging party with a wonderful corage, and killed mo of them than they did of the English men. Yet were there vi Scottes yn number to one English man, and came so sore on the communes of England that they began to fly;" but at that moment Thomas Grey was taken prisoner.

The castle remained but a short time in Scottish hands, for it was restored in May 1328, when the treaty of Northampton, recognising formally the independence of Scotland, had been ratified, and in this crowning act of Bruce's life, we still have proof how essential was the part which the old castle played in the fortunes of both countries.

Though successful in the Wear country, "a fresh foray on Northumberland forced the English court to submit to peace."*

"In 1327, soon after their flight from Weardale, the Scots laid siege to Norham, and took it by storm."†

We thus see that the last act of the Scotch war of independence was the capture of Norham, and the

* Green's "History of the English People," p. 208.
† "Hutchinson's "History of the Palatinate," vol. iii. p. 400.

crowning act of Bruce's life was the recognition of his sovereignty obtained through that capture.

The Baliol and the Bruce had disputed each other's claim before Norham in 1299. The Bruce had asserted his, and the independence of Scotland at Norham in 1328.

CHAPTER IX.

EDWARD III.

> "Goes your complaint to this? that we display
> A tale unsuited to the modern day?
> Does this fam'd island then produce no more
> The bright achievements of the days of yore?
> Avert the thought! still ancient glory's towers
> And warm heroic virtue still is ours!
> —*Edward Jerningham*, 1794, "*Siege of Berwick.*"

EARLY in June 1329, feeling that his death was fast approaching, King Robert Bruce—" good King Robert," as his people were wont to call him—summoned his best friends and counsellors to his bedside at Cardross, near Dumbarton, and after recommending his son David, a boy five years old, to their care, expressed the hope that, should his marriage with Joan Makepeace (a nickname given to the beautiful girl, sister of Edward III., because her betrothal was one of the conditions of the Treaty of Northampton) not turn out fruitful of issue, the crown might devolve on his grandson Robert, son of his daughter Marjory, who had married Walter, Lord High Steward of Scotland.

He then recommended (1) that when " they should

again have chance of wars with England, they would avoid set battles, and never hazard their all upon the fortune of one field, but keep off the enemy by frequent skirmishes, brisk onsets, and sudden incursions, and (2) that henceforth they should not make any lasting peace nor any truce longer than three or four years with England."*

Then turning to the "black" Douglas, he committed his heart to his care, to be taken by him to the Holy Land. On the 7th of June he died.

True to his friend and sovereign, Douglas set out for Palestine, but "was cast by storm of weather upon the coast of Spain, and forced to go ashore on the borders of Granada."† Here he at once joined Alphonso, King of Leon and Castile, who was at war with the Moors of Granada.

During a keen engagement with the latter, the old warrior, who carried the king's heart embalmed and put into a box of gold tied to a string round his neck, impatient of distinction, threw the gold casket among the Moors, crying out, "Onward as thou wert wont, thou noble heart! Douglas will follow thee;" but he was slain, and his body having been recovered as well as the heart in the gold casket, they were taken back to their native Scotland, and from this time

* "Martial Atchievements," vol. i. p. 639.

† "Life of Good Sir James, 1st James and 8th Lord of Douglas." David Hume, 1748. Vol. i. p. 95.

permission was given to the Douglas family to wear a crowned heart in their coat-of-arms.

As Bruce had anticipated, peace with England was of no long duration.

The Baliols were again at work, and had got round the martial King Edward, the illustrious father of the Black Prince.

On the 12th of April 1333, the king appeared before Berwick, the possession of which he had determined upon, and which was commanded by Sir William Keith and Sir Alexander Seton.

On the 19th of July, forgetting the wise and dying recommendations of their late king, the Scotch "hazarded their all upon the fortune of one field." The battle of Halidon Hill, long memorable as one of the most disastrous incidents in the annals of Scotland, decided the fate of Berwick, which from that day has remained a portion of English soil, and at the cost of some of Scotland's best blood, told in its results of the loss which Scotland had experienced by the death of Bruce.

"Seven earls, 900 knights, 400 esquires, and 32,000 men" are said to have died on the field of battle before the stout old Border town was abandoned by the Scotch.

It was then that the incident took place at Tweedmouth, at a place which still is called "Hang a dyke nook," which caused the life of the two young Setons, sons of Sir Alexander Seton, Scotch governor of Berwick, and which has been the subject of many ballads and plays, and of still more strictures upon the faithlessness of Edward III.*

By the year 1342, David Bruce had reconquered his territories from Baliol, excepting Berwick, and marched to Durham, where he spared neither clergy nor sacred edifices. Edward, however, followed him on his return to Scotland, and reached Wark, which was gallantly held by the Countess of Salisbury.

It was then and at Wark† that the Order of the

* A poem on this subject, written in 1794 by an ancestor of mine, was re-edited last year for the people of Berwick.

† Wark, or Werk, Anglice work, or "the honour of Carham," as it is called in old MSS., was after Bamborough one of the earliest fortified places of which the Saxon annals make mention; but its strength dates only of the time when the feudal barons of the Conquest believed their homes to be so many forts which they were obliged to defend, and which everybody envied, and though existing as a defensive settlement before Norham was thought of, it was only erected into a stronghold a few years after its "eastern" sister, A.D. 1158.

Thus the Dacres had their castle at Naworth, the Umfrevilles at Prudhoe, and the de Vesci at Wark.

Bamborough was strengthened in 1131.

Mitford was erected in 1150.

Norham in 1121.

Harbottle in 1155.

Naworth in 1280, and

Alnwick about 1130.

As, however, a special licence was required for the towers to be crennelled, that is, for archers to shoot from small apertures, it is no wonder that public fortresses had prior right to private

Garter is said to have been instituted. Lady Salisbury happening to drop her garter, the king picked it up, presented it to her, and seeing his courtiers smile, turned round upon them, saying, " Honi soit qui mal y pense," cleverly adding, " Shortly you shall see that garter advanced to so high an honour and renown as to account yourselves happy to wear it."

But though possible and even probable, the story has not the additional value of being strictly corroborated by history either in the category of facts or in the testimony of contemporary writers.

The neighbourhood of Wark to Norham justifies the legend finding its place here.

In 1546 took place the great battle of Neville's Cross, near Durham, where David was made the prisoner of Henry de Percy, though he had surrendered himself to one who was not even a knight, a certain John de Coupland of Coupland Manor, within the barony of Wooler.

This distinguished soldier, who was awarded a pension of £500 a year out of the customs of London and Berwick, received a moiety of the lands of Wooler, and also the shrievalty of Northumberland;

residences, and that Norham should thus be the oldest of them all. The reader will find interesting details as to Wark in a monograph by the Rev. Peter Mearns of Coldstream, and is specially referred to a remarkable and searching article on border fortresses in the Proceedings of the Archæological Institute," 1852, vol. ii.

and his old castle, which was destined later to receive fugitive royalty within its walls, is now the property of Mr M. Culley.

In 1355, the action at Nisbit Moor, won by the Scotch, so irritated Edward III. that he returned from France, arriving at Newcastle for Christmas ; he proceeded to Scotland on the following day, laying all Lothian waste, committing Edinburgh and Haddington to the flames, and received from Baliol a formal surrender of all his rights to the crown of Scotland.

David Bruce was still a captive in London, but in 1357 he received permission to return, and from that moment to his death in 1371, what might be called peace in those days reigned between England and Scotland.

At his death Robert Stewart succeeded, in accordance with the wish of Robert Bruce, and in 1377, on the 31st of June, Edward III. was gathered to his fathers.

His death was the signal for further warfare on the Borders. Roxburgh was burnt by the Scotch, Norham village was burnt. The Duke of Lancaster ingloriously invaded Scotland. Richard I. himself, advanced to Edinburgh, and the Scots in retaliation overran Cumberland and Durham.

* Queen Margaret, the wife of Henry VI., after the battle of Northampton, 1460.

At last, in 1388, the battle of Otterburn,* celebrated by the moonlight encounters between the Earl

* " It fell about the Lammas tide,
    When husbandmen do win their hay,
  Earl Douglas is to the English woods,
    And a' with him to fetch a prey.

  Earl Douglas to the Montgomery said,
    'Take thou the vanguard of the three,
  And bury me by the braken bush
    That grows upon yon lilye lee.'

  The Percy and Montgomery met,
    That either of other were fain,
  They swapped swords and they twa swat,
    And aye the blude ran down between.

  This deed was done at Otterburne,
    About the breaking of the day;
  Earl Douglas was buried at the braken bush,
    And the Percy led captive away."

Mr Robert White has written a very interesting history of the battle of Otterburn, and after a good deal of research fixes the spot where the battle began to be the farm of Greendesters, and that where the main struggle took place and terminated to be the farm of Townhead, on the east side of the Otter in the Davysheil district, near a wood and only a short distance from the ancient trackway from Newcastle to Scotland through Elsden by the Breken Moss.

In the list of English and Scotch warriors which he gives, we find the names of Hotspur—

"Schere Henry, quhat makis you to be
Sa werelike as yow now we se?"

because perhaps

"He had byn a Marchman all his dayes,
And kepte Barwyke upon Twede,"

of Douglas and Hotspur, the grandson of Henry, 1st Earl of Northumberland, in which Douglas was killed and Hotspur taken prisoner, was succeeded by the death in the following year of Robert II., and the accession of his son John, Earl of Carrick, known as Robert III., "the name of John having become odious to the Scottish people, who associated with it the

though

"Speaking thick, which nature made his blemish."

Sir Ralph Percy, Hotspur's brother.
Sir Robert Ogle.
Sir Thomas Umfreville.
Sir Robert Umfreville, his brother—

"Robin mend market."

Sir Thomas Grey of Heton, governor of Norham.
Walter Skirlawe, Bishop of Durham.
William, Lord Hilton.
Sir Matthew Redman.
Sir John de Lilburn.
Sir Aylmer de Athol, Lord of Jesmond and Ponteland,

and of

James, Earl of Douglas and Mar.
George, Earl of Dunbar and March.
The Earl of Moray.
Sir James Lindsay of Crawford.
Sir David Lindsay, Lord of Glenesk.
Sir Alexander Ramsay of Dalhousie.
Sir John de Montgomery of Eglesham.
Sir Patrick Hepburn of Hales.
Sir John Swinton de Swinton.
Sir Henry Preston.
Sir William de Dalzell.

memory of John Baliol, the special object of popular hatred.

A period of eight years followed this accession without, "mirabile dictu," the peace between the two countries being infringed, and it may generally be said that throughout the fifteenth century the history of the Borders is one of predatory warfare, carried on with unremitting energy rather by factions and rebellious subjects than by kings, despite repeated efforts to obtain peace, and innumerable truces which, in accordance with Bruce's advice, were never kept for "longer than three or four years when sued for by the Scots," or for much longer time when asked by the English.

The old castle during all this time was never attacked, its impregnable strength being asserted, and all the documents in connection with it only tell how its governors were paid, how its repairs were conducted, and the cost of these repairs.

Thus in 1382 Sir John Heron was paid " £50 for guarding the Castle of Norham, William de Eland, £3, 6s. 8d. for masonry work, and John de Kent, the bishop's messenger, 13s. 4d. for going to Norham with a letter from Bishop Fordham," of whom we read that "he was so deeply engaged in affairs of state that he had little time to attend particularly to the duties of his bishopric."

He, however, sanctioned the expenditure of 12s. on

ten sheaves of arrows without heads, and the purchase at Gateshead of twenty-four bows for the sum of 18s., the cost of their carriage being 8d.

In 1404, during the rebellion of the Percies, caused more by the fact that they could not get their outlays in the king's service repaid to them than by any other disloyal motive, Bishop Skirlaw, "whose life was occupied in works of munificence," appears to have given the watchers at Norham 1d. a night in addition to their ordinary wages, and an agreement entered into by the bishop and Robert de Ogle, their governor, is stated to have cost 6s. 8d., which was paid to the clerk who wrote it out.

This agreement is interesting, inasmuch as the Ogles, who had now come to the fore as one of the great families of Northumberland, were evidently intent on war, and discontented with their defensive position at Norham.

In the year 1403, on the 2d February, Robert de Ogle, son of Sir Robert de Ogle, knight, had been appointed Constable of Norham, justice, seneschall, and sheriff escheator in Norhamshire and Islandshire for seven years. In September he was appointed to the office for life, and was thus free to delegate his duties to a lieutenant while he sought fame elsewhere.

This Ogle was the sixth in descent of Sir Thomas de Hoggel, who came into notice in 1240, and whose subsequent heirs appear until the Robert Ogle of

Norham to have applied themselves very cleverly in putting the old Latin saying about Austria into practice—

"Bella dum gerant alii tu felix Austria nube,
Namque Mars aliis dat tibi regna Venus."

What with the marriages of his ancestors and his own, he was possessed at his death of no less than six castles and thirty-five manors and tenements.

His son became the first Lord Ogle, and he himself was a most distinguished administrator and soldier.

His descendants are still bearing the name in Northumberland.

In the same year, 1404, the accounts show that the governor was an energetic constable.

Twenty-four "flekys" or hurdles, costing 4s., were bought for the outer bridge of the castle; 3s. 4d. were paid to divers men who repaired the outer bridge; also various sums for repairing "the hall, the great chamber, all the chambers, the kitchen, and all the towers," and for bringing a sufficient stream to the mill of Bowden, and examining all the heads of the streams.

Again we find that the west gate of the castle was rebuilt from the ground in 298 days, from the 16th February 1408 to the 8th of December, and that William Caton was the clerk of the works, and the masons were William de Priors, William Spilbery, Robert Bank, and Walter de Scremerstone.

In 1422, as Sir Robert Umfreville, Governor of

M

Berwick, "with an army composed only of men of the palatinate and Northumbrians, in retaliation of the injuries received by the Scotch incursions," carried fire and sword through Teviotdale, burning all the Eastern March, with its market towns of Hawick, Selkirk, Jedburgh, Dunbar, and Lauder, the very year that Henry V., the hero of Agincourt (1415) was dying in France, Thomas Langley, Lord Chancellor of England and Bishop of Durham, gave instructions to Sir Robert de Ogle to build a new tower within the castle; and we find accordingly that Robert Fekenham, mason, got £22 for his share of the work; that Robert Shirwent, "quawrreour," and his associates, received £20, 16s. for winning stone in the quarry; that Robert Watson was paid £6, 4s. 8d. for carting, buying and burning lime, and that every door and window received new iron bars and bolts.

On his return from his raid into Roxburghshire, Sir Robert Umfreville stayed at Norham, a place which during his captaincy of Berwick he often visited, he and Ogle being such friends that, in the language of those days, they shared both "bed and meat."

Sir Robert Umfreville is particularly interesting to Northumbrians as the last of the celebrated family who bore that illustrious name.

He was a Knight of the Garter, a Vice-Admiral of England, and Lord of Redesdale, at the death of his nephew Gilbert, Earl of Kyme, slain in Anjou in 1421.

The admiral was not married, and at his death in 1436, the estates passed into the family of Talboys; but as if the Umfrevilles, to whom the Conqueror had given the lordship of Redesdale in 1076, and who for four centuries had been distinguished in both their male and female members, were to continue so in those who might succeed to their lands if not to their name, the lordship of Redesdale has ever since continued in the possession of families of distinction. King Henry VIII., on the demise of George, Lord Talboys, got possession of Redesdale in 1539; George, Lord Hume, Earl of Dunbar, on the accession of James I. of England, succeeded to it; the Howards of Corby purchased it in 1640 from the Earls of Suffolk; and in 1750 it was bought of William Howard by Sir Hugh Smithson, a Yorkshire baronet of old standing, who married Lady Elizabeth Seymour, the grandchild and heiress of the last of the Percies, and who in 1766 assumed by Act of Parliament the surname and arms of Percy, and was created Duke of Northumberland.

In 1425, John Daunce was paid 30s. for two cords of hemp, one of them 25 yards long, bought at Doncaster, for the works at Norham; and Thomas Smyth of Durham, "who worked 60 stones of my lord's iron into nails for the Castle of Norham, at 4½d. a stone, received 22s. 6d."

In 1429 the accounts show that some new "latrinæ" were commenced near to the great tower on the west, and were not finished till 1433.

Among other work done was a great doorway of stone under the vault of the dungeon of the great tower, in which an iron door was placed, and a new outhouse was built within the outer ward near the west gate, to be occupied, "half of it by the cart oxen, and the other by the masons when at work."

Sharpening 500 pikes and 100 axes cost 8s. 4d., while six extra pikes or axes cost 2s.

Lime brought from Shoreswood by Thomas Williamson was paid 13s. 4d. as the price of carting, and winning a coal pit at Bukton cost 45s. 3d.

In 1431 we have other interesting particulars as to the price of corn and coal.

Thus coal cost 1s. 4d. per chaldron (53 cwt.), or about 4s. of our present money.

Eight quarters, five bushels of wheat came to £2, 3s. 2½d., or 5s. a quarter, which is equivalent to 14s. a quarter present value.

Seventeen quarters, three bushels of barley was paid £4, 7s. 10½d., or £52, 14s. 6d. current coin, which shows barley to have been sold then in actual currency at about 14s. 1d. a quarter.

In the same year, James Strangways, Christopher Boynton, esquires; Sir John Woodryngton, knight;

Sir John Bertram, knight; Sir John Middleton, knight; William Chauncellor, William Strothes, John Cartington, and Robert Whelpyngton, appointed commissioners of assize, justices of the peace, and commissioners of gaol delivery in Norham and Islandshire, arrived at Norham Castle, and were the guests of the constable.

The cost and expenses of these gentlemen, who only stayed a day and a half, but who had brought with them twenty-two horses, was only 42s., which, at the rate of £2, 16s. to the £ sterling, is equivalent to £5, 18s. of our money.

In 1476, William Dudley was appointed Bishop of Durham, and in the very month of his installation, one Alexander Lee Clerk was commissioned by King Edward IV. to examine into the repairs at Norham, and was accompanied by John Asseby, secretary to Bishop Dudley, and Thomas Metcalf, the bishop's auditor. The latter was commissioned also to make a survey and valuation of the bishop's lands in Norhamshire. The expenses of all three for ten days appear to have been altogether £5, 6s. 8d. or £14, 18s. 8d.

In 1491, John Johnson was paid 6s. 8d. for the carriage to Newcastle from Auckland of two "fother of lead" for the castle of Norham; and in 1493, while the Bishopric of Durham was vacant, Henry VII. appointed Sir Thomas Gray, captain and receiver of Norham, with orders to pay £80 to the next Bishop of Durham.

Richard Fox was appointed bishop, and he appointed Thomas Garth captain of the castle of Norham, with one Hamerton as his lieutenant.

In the year 1496, James IV. of Scotland avowed himself a supporter of Perkin Warbeck, whom he either looked upon, or for purposes of his own chose to look upon, as Richard, Duke of York, the legitimate heir to the throne and brother to the queen, who had married Henry VII., and thereby put an end to the disastrous War of the Two Roses.

Having this Perkin in his company, James invaded England with a powerful army, declaring that "he wald onely forbeir to invaid the boundis quha wold assist to Richard, Duik of York and none uther . . . bot seing that no Inglisheman did resort to the saide Richard, nochtwithstanding of the gret extremitie used, returned agane within his awin cuntrey of Scotland, and considering that the said Richardes promesseis of the assistance of his frindes followed not in deid according to his wordis, causit the king to chaunge the guid opinione quhilk he had of him ; and this wes the occasione of the beginning of great weir betwixt the tua realmes." *

Henry VII. raised an army, and placed it under the command of Lord Dawbeny, but other troubles postponed its march northwards, and meanwhile James IV. appeared in person before Norham.

* Lesley of Ross's " History of Scotland," vol. i. p. 64.

For fifteen days the new and murderous engines of war were brought to bear against the old castle, * but the valour of Garth and of Hamerton were better than stone balls and scaling ladders.

So gallant was the fight that at the end of a fortnight the shouts of the little garrison proclaimed the raising of the siege, and the departure of the Scottish king and his great army.

"In persoun with his army did the king causit siege the castell of Norame, qwhilk was then weill furneisit be Richard Fox, Bishop of Durame, with men, munition and victuallis, quhair he lay long tyme at the siege thereof; bot seing that he couth not win the same, albeit that he had done great domage and skaith thereto, he returnit within his realme, and left greit cumpanyes of men upon the boundouris for defence of the samyn."

---

* It was at this siege that "Mons Meg," a cannon from the Mons Foundry in Belgium, was supposed to have been used, but I am of opinion it was not brought to bear against the walls until the second siege by James IV. immediately before Flodden; and am the more convinced of this, that, as the following chapter will show, it was not till after this first siege which Edward undertook on the Borders, more with the intention of giving time to Perkin Warbeck's friends to rally round him, as he had assured King James they would if once he took up the offensive, than with any intention of invading England, that James IV. received numerous presents of arms and munition from France and Belgium. It is true, however, that "Mons Meg" was cast in 1476, and might easily have been used therefore at the earlier siege.

Meanwhile the bishop appealed to the Earls of Surrey and Northumberland to come to the relief of Norham, but as the Bishop of Ross quaintly puts it, "on the cumming thereto, the king and his army were departit."

Garth had won the day, and an annuity of five marks for life was granted by the bishop to Thomas Garth and John Hamerton, "for their strenuous defence of the castle of Norham, when besieged for fifteen days by James, King of Scotland in person, 19th August 1498." *

We are hurrying to the days of Flodden, and the historical life of Norham is ebbing fast. This last gallant resistance of the impregnable fortress is like the flickering of a light which must soon die out, but before it goes out completely, from Norham Castle comes the little incident which is to bear the fruit of Scottish and English Union.

* 4 Fox, Rot. A., 22.

CHAPTER X.

MARRIAGE OF JAMES IV.

> "Take with thee thy dower,
> Britain's best blood, and beauty ever new,
> Being of mind; may the cool northern dew
> Still rest upon thy leaves, transplanted flower."
> —*Lord Houghton.*

THE events which precede Flodden, read by the light of history, point very significantly to a desire on the part of the Scotch turbulent nobility, if not on that of the politic James IV. himself, to avail themselves of an opportunity of waging war upon England, the condition of which was weaker than at almost any other period of her history.

The bloody contest known as the War of the Two Roses had not been waged against property but against men. Towns, villages, crops, and homesteads had been respected, and commerce indeed had developed, but the blood of English nobles had been spilled with reckless prodigality and cruelty.

The working classes were not fighting classes, but left this occupation to their betters! And what better cause could these dying remnants of a chivalrous age find to fight for than to give England another king, "albeit they already had one,"—because John of Gaunt had by his mistress, Catherine Swynford, a Lancaster descendant in Beaufort, Duke of Somerset, and the Duke of York was a descendant of the fifth son of Edward the Third. Henry VI. was still on the throne; and with pitiless good sense, at the very time he was supposed to be insane, he asked how his right could be disputed, "his father having been king, his grandfather also, himself having worn the crown forty years from his cradle, and all these nobles now ,clamouring having sworn fealty to him, representative of the House of Lancaster."

For thirty years, however, the adherents of the white rose of York slew, murdered, and butchered, or were slain, murdered, and butchered, by those who preferred the red rose of Lancaster; and the result was that when at last common sense prevailed, and the two badges were united in the person of Henry VII. by his marriage with Elizabeth of York, the fighting element of England was at its lowest ebb, and the country was open to any invader.

No wonder then that James IV., who could not ever really have believed in the claims of Perkin Warbeck to be the brother of the boy murdered in the Tower, since he was well aware that the Yorkists in England entirely repudiated this Flemish impostor, found it politic to convert him into an instrument for political uses in the promotion of the warlike aims of his nobles, and to give some colour to his belief in him by marrying him to Lady Katherine Gordon, the daughter of Lord Huntly.

Even in those days the brutal murder of Edward V. in the Tower had caused great commotion throughout Europe, and it is not to be wondered at that the old Duchess of Burgundy should have been gulled into the belief that Perkin Warbeck was the brother of the murdered child.

She gave him special letters of recommendation to James IV.; and as an alliance with France under certain circumstances was a very desirable object to attain, no wonder again that the King of Scots received with favour a *protégé* of France.

Again, the ease with which the chivalrous James gave up the cause of his friend, and the long time he tarried with him before Norham without ostensible cause, all show that Warbeck was in his hands a good political weapon rather than an accepted claimant to a throne, an alliance with which may even then have been crossing his mind.

Be this as it may, James IV. received a rude shock when, after his unsuccessful attempt on Norham, he found that the rebellious north, so ready usually to enter upon the game of war,

"For war is the Borderer's game,"

refused to join his ranks or the pretender's banner.

A truce was concluded at Melrose by Bishop Fox on behalf of King Henry; and though James IV.

refused to give up Perkin Warbeck, "as ane that trublit the quietness of the realme of England," because " he esteemed his honour mair precious nor any other thing," he agreed "that the saide Richard, Duik of York, suld be sent furth of the realme of Scotland, and nocht to be resett thaireftir."

Warbeck thanked the king and was not slow to leave Scotland, intending, as he said, to go to Ireland with his wife; but he was taken in the sanctuary of Bewdeley, pardoned with his life, and expelled the country.

King Henry seeing the Lady Catherine's beauty, "thought her a prey more mete for an emperor than a soldier, and therefore sent her with a company of honourable women to the queen, who entertained her well at the king's desire, and she was afterwards known in England as the white rose of Scotland, and lived there very honourably for many years thereafter."

While these incidents in the life of Perkin Warbeck and his wife were taking place, a "sudden discord betwixt certain young Scotchmen of the Borders and the keepers of the Castle of Norham" occurred which, as the Scotch historian Lesley says, "almaist had renewit the wearis betuix the said tua realmes."

While the feeling at Norham was still running high, and the guardians and garrison of the castle still kept a vivid remembrance of their fourteen days' siege a little more than a year before, it happened that certain Scotchmen, having crossed the Tweed for sake of plunder, "albeit that menit na fraude nor evill," were observed from the castle, near which they strayed incautiously, whereupon a number of soldiers issued from the castle, gave them chase, killed many and wounded some.

The incident* was a trifling one, and matter for judgment before the courts rather than for political notice, as the Scotch marauders were caught "flagrante delicto," and, but for the feeling of the day, should have been captured and delivered up to justice.

But on the matter being reported to King James, then staying at Melrose, he was much incensed; and declaring "that there was nothing more uncertain than the maintenance of peace with England," despatched at once sharp and angry letters to King Henry, who replied, somewhat satirically as was natural, that the

* Hutchinson gives another version: "An accident which happened about this time was near destroying what had been effected with so much attention. In the intercourse which immediately took place between the people of both nations on the borders, some Scottish youths came upon a party of pleasure to Norham. The garrison thought they were too speculative, and paid too near attention to the works of the castle, considering the recent hostilities between the states. The sentinels, in a manner offensive to the Scots, prevented their curiosity, and a fray began in which some were slain."—Hutchinson's "Antiquities of Durham," vol. i, p. 374.

"condign punishment of these Scotchmen was not by his counsall nor command," but rather due to the rash and venturous spirit of the keepers of Norham, that therefore the truce was in no wise violated or broken, but that to show his good faith and spirit of amity he would shortly take knowledge of the case, and should any of his subjects be found guilty, he would have them duly punished.

The Bishop of Durham wrote in the same strain to King James. "I regret," said he, "that through the occasion of my men who guard the Castle of Norham, which appertains to this bishopric, trouble should arise again between England and Scotland, and I beg you to accept 'mendis for the injuris done, quilk suld be reparit at your pleasour.'"

King James, "considering the wisdom, faithfulness, and gravity" of Bishop Fox, sent satisfactory answers to the bishop, and also to the king's letters; while he expressed a hope that the bishop would find time to come to Melrose, talk the incident over, and discuss with him "uther matters."

Fox, who is said to have been "a man of considerable political abilities, and appears to have been more of the artful statesman than of the Christian prelate," guessing the purport of the "uther matters," at once applied to King Henry for leave to be his plenipotentiary in Scotland, and to repair to Melrose; an application which received the royal assent as soon as it was made.

To Melrose Bishop Fox repaired early in 1500, after spending a night at Norham, and hearing from Thomas Garth himself the details of the affray which had so much displeased the King of Scotland.

At Melrose he was received with all due honours, and lodged in the abbey, and after a first meeting with one who, in the king's opinion, "had such power to charm his passions and silence his wrath," James IV. expressed himself satisfied with the measures proposed by the "wise bishop" for the redress of the wrongs he complained of, and then "revealed to him the secret of his bosom."

In strict secrecy and confidence, the king declared to Fox "the guid will and mynd quhilk he had to intertayne perpetuall frindschip with King Henry, and wald wische the same to knit, that it mycht in na wayis be dissolvit agane."

The surest way, thought the king, would be for the King of England to give him his eldest daughter in marriage, and to obtain this end he was ready to send ambassadors to England; but before acting on this notion he expressed himself anxious to have the bishop's advice, "for he wolde be loth to desire that thing quhilk suld be refusit."

The bishop remarked that although a dispensation would be required from the pope, owing to the princess' youth and the degree of relationship which already existed between the two courts, he clearly entered into the views of the king, and was in good hopes of cementing the alliance between the two countries in the manner suggested.

Anxious to obtain the credit of this alliance, which was to bear such fruits in future times, Bishop Fox hurried back to London, where he found King Henry, and reported to him the result of his interviews.

"The King of England, quha hering his proceedingis, and being glaid thairwith, causit the saide bischop adverties the King of Scottis to send his ambassadouris for the effect above written."

Upon this an embassy, composed of the Archbishop of Glasgow, of Patrick Hepburn of Crichton, first Earl of Bothwell—

> "'Twas a brave race before the name
> Of hated Bothwell stain'd their fame"—

and other noblemen, was despatched to London to ask the hand of Margaret Tudor for their king.

On their arrival a council was summoned, and the Bishop of Durham, together with the Scotch ambassadors, was present.

Remarks were made which were not altogether complimentary to Scotland, and show how strong the feeling still was against it, since the contingency of a Scotch prince having at some future day any right to the throne of England by reason of the proposed marriage appears to have frightened some of the king's advisers, who believed it to be a lesser evil for the king to marry the princess to a foreigner.

The prophetic tone of the king's reply is also particularly noteworthy and interesting :—

"Some of the counsellouris did prepone certane ressonis for staying of the saide marriage, allegeing that it mycht happin that the heretage and successioun of the realme of Ingland mycht fall to Margaret, his eldest dochter, and to her successioun of her body, and thairfor semit best that she should be maricit apoun ane forane prince."

King Henry thereupon replied, "What then if such things did happen ?—which God forbid ! I see that it would come to this, that our realme would receive no damage therefrom ; for in that case England would not accrue to Scotland, but Scotland would accrue to England, as to the most noble head of the whole island. For at that time the thing which is least is used to be joined to that thing which is greatest, to the honour of the same ; even as when Normandy came into the power of Englishmen, our forefathers."

The wise reply was much commended and approved, the immediate result being that the Lady Margaret was "granted unto the King of Scotland, and certain contracts and indentures were made," furnished with which the Scotch commissioners returned to Scotland "with great comfort," 1501.

A treaty of peace and amity, to last the lives of

both kings, was signed at the same time, and in the following year (1502) the marriage contract was ratified by the same persons who had been sent before to arrange about the marriage. It was stipulated that Margaret should receive as a jointure a sum equivalent to £6000 Scots, and a dowry of 30,000 nobles of gold, or about £10,000, and that she should be delivered at Berwick, which was to remain for ever an integral portion of the English realm, into the hands of her future husband's representatives.

On the 25th day of January 1502, Earl Bothwell, "as commissioner and by mandate in the name of King James, his master, contractit and handfastit*

---

* The ceremony of hand-festing, which consisted in the right hands of the contracting couple being joined in the presence of the priest, was a remnant of Danish days, and was the occasion of the public avowal of the intention of a couple to become man and wife.

In an old publication of the year 1543, forty years after the time of which we are writing, there is this remark, which shows that people who had once hand-fested were not so prone to get married :—

" After the handfastynge and makyng of the contract ye church going and beddyng shuld not be deferred too longe, lest the wicked sow his ungracious seed in the mean season. Into this dish hath the devil put his foot, and mingled it with many wicked uses and customs."*

At Eskdalemuir, in Dumfries, there was an annual fair, and " at that fair it was the custom for the unmarried persons of both sexes to choose a companion according to their liking, with whom they were to live till that time next year. This was called hand-

* "Popular Antiquities." Brand & Ellis. Vol. ii., p. 20.

the saide fair lady publictlie, at Sanct Paul's croice in Lundoun, with great rejoicing and triumphe in the kirk, and great fires made through the whole city of Lundoun."

Leland, from whom most of the following interesting narrative of the Princess Margaret's betrothal and journey to Scotland is taken, and who gives as his authority a manuscript written by John Younge, Somerset Herald, who attended the princess on her journey, mentions the ceremony above described by Bishop Lesley as having taken place at St Paul's, in London, to have been held "on St Paul's Day in the king's royal manor of Richmond."

Having heard mass and a "notable sermon made by the reverend fader the Lorde Richard Fitz James, Bishop of Chichester," the bridal party repaired to the queen's chamber, where the Earl of Surrey "well and right sadly, with very good manner," declared the cause of the present assemblage.

Dr Ruttall, the king's secretary, then read publicly the commission of the Scotch ambassadors; a canon of Glasgow, Mr David Coningham, read the pope's

---

fasting, or hand in fist. If they were pleased with each other at that time, then they continued together for life; if not, they separated, and were free to make another choice as at the first. A priest came from time to time from the Abbey of Melrose to marry the couples, and he was called Book-i'-bosom, because he carried the book with him wherein to register the marriage."*

* "Popular Antiquities." Brand & Ellis. Vol. ii., p. 20.

bulls of dispensation "for consanguinity, affinity, or nonage;" the Archbishop of Glasgow asked the king whether His Grace knew of any impediment, and also the queen, and also the princess, and all three having replied "there was none," the same question was put to the Scotch ambassadors by the king, who besides asked the Earl of Moray "whether it was the very will and mind of the King of Scots and full intent that the said Earl Bothwell should in his name affiance the said princess?"

This having been answered in the affirmative, the princess herself was required to say whether "she were content without compulsion and of her free will?"

She then answered, "If it please my lord and father the king, and my lady my mother the queen," whereupon she received the king and queen's blessing.

Then were read the words by which Patrick, Earl of Bothwell, "having sufficient authority, power, and commandment to contract matrimony, 'per verba de presenti,'" in the name of his sovereign lord did "contract matrimony with thee Margaret, and take thee unto and for the wife and spouse of James, King of Scotland," plighting his faith and troth thereto.

Margaret did the same, the trumpeters sounded a merry note, "and the loud noise of minstrells played in the best and most joyfullest manner."

Banquets and tournaments minutely described

followod this ceremony, and the Earl of Bothwell presented to the officers at arms the gown of gold cloth that "he wore when he was fyanced," besides a hundred crowns.

A year elapsed after this, during which time the young princess remained with her parents at Richmond in strict retirement.

On the 27th of June, however, 1503, King Henry VII., accompanied by his daughter, proceeded to Coliveston in Northamptonshire, on a visit to the Countess of Richmond, Margaret's grandmother.

On the 8th of July, the king parted affectionately with his daughter, confiding her to the charge of the Earl of Surrey, treasurer of England, who was to deliver her into the hands of the King of Scots, and accompany her throughout the journey.

Surrey was the son of Jock of Norfolk, who fell gallantly fighting for his friend Richard III. on Bosworth field; and little did he think when escorting this young and blooming girl of fourteen to the court of James, that he was destined to defeat that king some ten years later, and make her a widow whom he was now hurrying to make a bride.

Many lords and ladies accompanied her to York, but Lord Hastyngs appears to have distinguished himself, for he is reported "to have done marvellously well on horseback in steering of his horse."

The princess was richly dressed and mounted on a

fair palfrey, and before her rode Sir Davy Owen, three footmen, "very honestly appointed," being always near her.

A little behind, two footmen, "arrayed as the others, conveyed a very rich litter borne by two fair coursers, in the which litter the said princess was borne when entering towns, or otherwise to her good pleasure."

Then came the ladies mounted, squires and gentlemen, then a chariot in which were the four ladies who had to travel the whole journey, then the gentlewomen attendant upon the ladies, then minstrels, trumpetters, officers of arms in their coats, sergeants-at-arms with their mace, and other retinue, "which was fair to see."

Half way to Grantham Sir Robert Dymock, Sheriff of Lincolnshire, met the princess and accompanied her with thirty horses in his livery to the limits of the county.

At Grantham she lodged "with a gentleman called Mr Hioll."

From Grantham she proceeded to Newark, the people on the way "bringing great vessels full of drink, and giving the same to them that need had of it, saying that if better they had had, better they should have brought."

At Newark "she lodged at the Hert," thence she proceeded to Tuxford and to Sirowsby, a place belonging to the Archbishop of York.

On the 13th of July Sir William Conyers, Sheriff of Yorkshire, arrived with sixty horses, and accompanied her to Doncaster, where she lodged at the Carmelites.

On the 14th she reached Pomfret, and lodged at the abbey.

On the 15th she proceeded to Tadcaster, where she was greeted by Lord Latimer and his wife and fifty horses.

On her leaving this place Lord Scrope of Bolton, Lord Scrope of Upsall, and twenty horses met her two miles out of the town, and two miles further Lady Conyers came with sixty horses to greet her.

When two miles from York, she was met by Henry Percy, Earl of Northumberland, Warden of the Marches, who with the Earl of Surrey was to deliver the princess into the hands of her future husband.

He rode a charger, on which was a cloth of crimson velvet, "all bordered with precious stones," his arms richly embroidered on his saddle and harness, his stirrups gilt, and himself arrayed in a gown of crimson, fringed at the collar and sleeves with stones of price.

Two footmen were by his side, and in his numerous suite were Sir John Hastings, Sir John Pennington, Sir Robert Aske, and a host of other gentlemen resplendent with gold and silver.

With him also was his officer-at-arms, called Northumberland Herald, arrayed in his livery of velvet, bearing the Percy arms on his surcoat.

According to the chronicler Hall, both Scotch and English who saw him "esteemed him more like a prince than a subject."

His memory has come down to posterity, not only as a man "of great magnificence and taste," but what is better still, as "a generous patron of learning and of genius."

This commendation is all the more creditable, that, in the words of the chronicler, "perhaps at no period of time were his brother peers in general more illiterate."

The princess' reception at York might form the subject of a whole volume, so interesting are the customs of those days, the dresses worn, and the pageants held in her honour.

Thomas Savage, Archbishop of York, of whom it is said "that he was more of courtier and a sportsman than of an ecclesiastic," the Lord Mayor, Sir John Guillott, "in satin crimson," and the aldermen in gowns of scarlet and gold chains, received the princess "very meekly" outside the town, and when the procession entered York, "all the windows were so full of nobles, ladies, gentlemen, damsels, burgesses, and others in so great multitude, that it was a fair sight for to see."

On the 16th, being Sunday, she heard mass in the minster, and the sight was magnificent.

After church the Countess of Northumberland was

presented to her, "the princess kissing her in the welcoming," and during dinner "trumpets and other instruments rang in the ancient manner."

On the 17th the princess left York for Newborough, where she slept at the priory.

On the 18th she went to Allerton, where she was conveyed to the manor house belonging to the Bishop of Durham.

On the 19th she moved on to Darneton under the conduct of Sir James Strangways, and thence to the village of Hexham under that of Lord Lumley and his sons.

Here she was met by Sir William Bulmer, with "six score horses," as captain of the Bishop of Durham's forces, and on the 20th reached Durham, outside which town Sir Edward Stanley and his wife met her.

At the entrance to the cathedral, to which she at once proceeded, she was greeted by Bishop Sinews, a Benedictine monk, who had succeeded Fox, created Bishop of Winchester, and by the Prior of Durham, dressed in their pontificals, after which she went to the castle, "where her lodging was prepared and dressed honestly."

She remained four days at Durham, "her costs being borne by the said bishop, who gave double dinner and double supper to all comers worthy to be there."

On the 24th she left Durham, and three miles outside Newcastle she was met by the Prior of Tynemouth with thirty horses, "all his folks in livery," and by Sir Ralph Harbotle with forty horses.

At Newcastle she was received by the Sheriff of Northumberland, Sir Henry Ewers; by the mayor, John Snow; the ex-mayor George Carr; the sheriff, Robert Baxter; the ex-sheriff, Thomas Hall, and all the aldermen, among whom were George Bird, Bartholomew Young, John Blaxton, Thomas Riddell, and John Brandling.

At the bridge end children dressed in white were singing hymns and playing various instruments.

The princess was conveyed to the Austin Friars, where she lodged the night.

On the following day arrived Lord Dacre and "his folks," who a few years later was to find the body of her dead husband on the field of Flodden.

On the 26th she left Newcastle for Morpeth, having been joined by Sir Humphrey Lisle and the Prior of Brinkburne.

On the 27th the princess went to Alnwick, and on her way thither was complimented by "Maister Henry Gray, Esquire, with his folks in his livery, to the number of one hundred horses."

Two miles from Alnwick the Earl of Northumberland, who had hurried before her from Newcastle, came to meet her, "well accompanied, and brought her through his park, where she killed a buck with her bow, after which she was conveyed to the castle, where she and her company were welcomed, the which made her very good cheer."

On the 29th she left Alnwick for Berwick, and stayed at Belford on the way, "for Sir Thomas d'Arcy, capitaine of Berwick, had made ready her dinner at the said place very well and honestly."

"Maister Henry Gray being Sheriff of Islandshire and Norhamshire, he bore his rod before the princess" until her entry into Berwick.

Betwixt Alnwick and Berwick she was accompanied by Sir Richard Cholmeley, Constable of Norham, by Sir Ralph Widdrington, and a hundred gentlemen of Northumberland, among whom were names well known in the present day—Thomas Haggerstone, Bertram Mitford, Nicholas Blenkinsop, Lancelot Ridley, Roger Fenwick, Ogle, Clavering, Orde, Collingwood, and Selby.

At Tweedmouth the pretty little princess alighted at the house of Sir William Tyler, who, on the 1st September 1491, had, for the sum of £27, 2s. a year,[*] leased "all the lands, tenements, rentes, houses, meadows, pastures, and arable lands lying within and about the town of Tweedmouth, together with all manner of fishing waters of Tweed, with the coal-mine."

[*] £75, 18s. of our money.

Tweedmouth was a portion of the Palatinate, and the above indenture had been signed by Bishop Fox of Durham.

After changing her riding apparel, the young princess, who was tired with her journey, albeit that at Belford she had "dined well and honestly," drove by the bridge to Berwick, and on arriving at the end of it she was received by Sir Thomas d'Arcy and a numerous company of gentlemen and men-at-arms.

Such was a royal procession in the days of merry England, and before railways were thought of.

Having tarried a couple of days in the old fortified Border town, to possess which more blood had been spilt of both English and Scotch than any other town in both countries, and therefore was more than any other place entitled to rejoice at the prospect of even a distant union of the two kingdoms, Margaret and her long train of splendidly attired knights entered Scotland, and proceeding to Lambertonkirk, four miles to the north of Berwick, was received by the Archbishop of Glasgow and by the Earl of Morton, who, with a pompous train, received the bride and conducted her to Fast Castle, from whence, on the 2nd of August, she proceeded to Haddington by Dunbar, "where on her passing they shot ordnance for the love of her."

"Great quantities of people assembled for to see their queen, bringing with them plenty of drink for each one that would have of it in paying therefore."

After a night's rest she proceeded to Dalkeith, called "Acquik" by Leland, where the Countess of Morton knelt before her, and the earl presented the keys of the castle, "welcoming her as lady and maitresse."

On the 3d of August King James arrived, "his lyre behind his back, his beard something long," and "head bare," kissed Margaret, "and likewise kissed the ladies and others also."

On the 4th the king, "flying as the bird that seeks its prey," came privately to Dalkeith, "where he found the queen playing at the cards," but on his entering "she kissed him of good will," and he only saluted the company present.

It were too long to tell all the rejoicings that took place,—how "Lord Gray led the queen to the dance;" how "the king played the lute, much to her pleasure;" how "Sir Edward Stanley sang a ballad;" how at supper the king gave the queen the chair on which he sat, "because the queen was not at her ease on a stool;" how the courtship progressing, the king and queen embraced, "without sparing courtesy;" how at last, unable to be separated from her, "he mounted the palfrey of the queen and she behind him, and so rode through the town of Edinburgh;" how there being two cushions in the church for the king and queen to kneel upon, the king "would never kneel first but both together;" and lastly, how, "holding always the queen by the body," he brought her to Holyrood.

The marriage was celebrated with extraordinary pomp and magnificence, and altogether this assemblage of the great knights of both countries must have been a most wonderful sight; for according to the Bishop of Ross, "the Scottis men at this tyme war nocht beheynd, bot far above the Inglis men baithe in appareill, rich juellis, and massive chains, and mony ladies having thair habilyemantis partly set with goldsmith work, garnished with precious stones, with their gallant and well-trappit horses, wer cumly to se."

Indeed, according to Rymer, "even foreigners came to attend the festival;" and "when all things were done and finist according to thair commission, the Earl of Surry, with all the Inglis lordis, returnit into thair country, geving greit praise not only to the manhood of the Scottish men, but also to thair guid manners and hartlie intertenyment which they receivit of them."

Thus was celebrated the marriage which, one hundred years after, was, in the words of the commissioners of Scotland to Henry the Seventh, "possibly to cause the succession of the realm of England to fall to the succession of the body of Margaret, his eldest daughter," and, in the king's words, " was not, even if this were to happen, to cause any damage to England thereby."

We may be excused for having tarried a little longer on this subject than perhaps the object of this volume might seem to warrant; but it must not be forgotten (besides the brief insight into the manners of the day) that any serious means of stopping Border warfare directly affected the standing purposes of Border fortresses, and in particular the object for which Norham had been built. So true is this, that within a very few years of the wedding which has just been related, Norham Castle ceased to have a history.

But it is ever to be remembered that whether or not the project of the marriage between King James, a young man twenty-five years of age, with a girl only twelve years old when he disclosed his object to Bishop Fox at Melrose, had been decided in his mind some time before, it was an ordinary broil caused by the impetuosity of the garrison of Norham Castle that brought about the negotiations for the marriage, and subsequently the marriage itself.

Thus from Norham came that seed of peace which was to unite England and Scotland in sympathy, in strength, and in unity of purpose against the world. Time and vandal hands have shorn the old Border castle of its strength and of its walls, but still the keep stands proudly forth in assertion of her old power, which generations have learnt to respect even since the days when she forced others to respect her, and the great tower with its side open towards Scotland appears to tell even now of the peace she won for England through the marriage of Margaret Tudor, while the still impregnable wall on the south seems to point to Englishmen of the present day how in times gone by she could uphold the might and honour of England's fame.

CHAPTER XI.

FLODDEN.

> " Now ballad, gather poppies in thine hands,
> And sheaves of brier and many rusted sheaves
> Rain-rotten in rank lands.
>
> . . . . . .
>
> Seek out Death's face ere the light altereth,
> And say, 'My master that was thrall to love
> Is become thrall to death.'"—*Swinburne.*

IN 1509 Henry VII. died, bequeathing the enormous sum for those days of two millions sterling to his son Henry VIII., together with the mad notion that England had rights upon the French crown, which must never be abandoned, as if nations in their development counted with mortals, be they kings or friars, and were to accept them as hereditary rulers against their will.

As a counterbalance to the power of France, Spain, under Ferdinand, had become a great state, and to secure her aid against France, Henry VIII. married Ferdinand's daughter, Catherine of Arragon, the widow of his eldest brother Arthur.

Watching the opportunity of spending the money left him by his sordid father, and of gratifying his ambitious views, Henry VIII. ratified the treaty of peace with Scotland, which had been signed by Henry

VII. in 1502, and being asked by Spain to join the league, which the Italian states with Pope Julius II. at their head had formed to expel Lewis XII. of France from Lombardy, Henry consented so as to secure the good-will of Ferdinand.

The aim of Ferdinand was really the conquest for himself of the French province of Navarre, and Henry soon found to his cost that he had only been made use of, and that he alone was to derive no benefit from the successful issue of the war waged by the league. Furious with the pope, with Ferdinand, with the French, with everybody, the impetuous Henry resolved upon invading France in person.

After taking leave of Catherine, he commanded the Earl of Surrey to draw towards the north, fearing the Scots would invade it in his absence, and constituted him lieutenant of all the northern provinces, empowering him to raise all men able to bear arms in the counties of Chester, Lancaster, Durham, Northumberland, Westmoreland, and Cumberland.

The Earl of Surrey then accompanied Henry to Dover, and here the king, taking Surrey's hand, said, "My lord, I trust not the Scots, therefore I pray you be not negligent;" to which Surrey answered, "I shall so do my duty that your grace shall find me diligent, and to fulfil your will shall be my gladness."

The chronicler Hall, from whom these particulars are gathered, went over to France in the same ship with Henry, and tells how Surrey could scarcely speak with emotion and concern at being left behind, and said to some around him, "Sorry shall I be if I don't see the King of Scots, who is cause of my abiding behind; but if ever we meet, I shall do that which lieth in me to make him as sorry as I now am, or die."

The king having embarked, Surrey returned to London, and attended on the queen, comforting her as best he could, and shortly sent for his gentlemen and tenants, five hundred able men, whom he mustered before Sir Thomas Lovel on July 21st. The following day he rode through London northward on his way to Doncaster.

Rumours by this time had reached him of the bellicose intentions of the Scotch, so he pushed on to Pomfret, where he had summoned the noblemen and gentlemen of the counties in his charge to meet him, and certify to him as to the number of able men, horsed and armed, they could raise at an hour's warning to attend him.

This was done on the 1st August, and posts "having been laid every way to advertise them," he sent a message to Sir Ralph Grey of Warke, and to Sir Richard Cholmeley, captain of Norham, informing them that "if in their opinion the castle of Norham was in any danger, he would be ready to relieve it."

Cholmeley, however, wrote back, "thanking the earl, and praying that the King of Scots would come with his puissance, for he would keep him in play till the King of England came out of France."

This reply reached Surrey a few days only before the 22d of August, when "the King of Scots did come before Norham with his puissance," just about the same time that Henry, who had landed in the north of France, and had routed the French cavalry at Guinegate (when their precipitate flight had shown the victor so many heels that the day was called the "battle of spurs"), was besieging Terouenne.

Events in Scotland during these early months had been hastening to a crisis, and the following (briefly told) will explain how it was that Henry on leaving England had some justification for his saying to the Earl of Surrey that he "trusted not the Scots."

A year before, in June 1512, one Andrew Barton, a sea-pirate, who was waging a little war of his own with Portugal, was returning to Scotland with his plunder, when in the Downs he encountered Sir Edmund Howard, Lord High Admiral of England, and son of Lord Surrey, who called upon him to surrender.

Barton refused, and an engagement took place, during which he was slain. His Scotch sailors were taken prisoners to London, and his two ships, the *Lyoun* and the *Jennypirryne*, were captured.

James IV. at once remonstrated against this breach of the peace between England and Scotland.

Henry replied that the capture of a Scotch pirate was no breach of the peace with Scotland, but that nevertheless to satisfy James he would send commissioners to the Borders to treat upon "that and all uther enormities betwixt the tua realmes."

Meanwhile France was looking everywhere for an ally, and already in 1506 she had sent a herald, le Sire de Montgommery, with overtures to James, who received him kindly, but promised nothing; and in 1512 she entrusted John, Lord Gordon, who had been Scotch ambassador at the French court, with a confidential message, which was communicated to the king's council.

As time was wearing on, and Henry's commissioners made no appearance according to promise, the capture of Barton's ships still remaining unredressed, James received openly M. de la Mote, who came over to persuade the King of Scotland to make war against England, promising him, if he did so, both money, munition, and war materiel on behalf of the French king.

James Ogilvy, Abbot of Dryburgh, arrived from France at the same time with still more pressing letters, and at the end of July 1512, de la Mote returned to France with the king's assurance of support in the manner desired by Louis XII.

In November following the king received "ane greit schip, send fra the King of France, full of artailyric, pulder, and wine," and in the following May 1513, four more laden with guns, powder, harness, and other kinds of ammunition.

All these were forwarded at once to the Tweed, and de la Mote, who had come over with them, was attached as ambassador to the staff of the king.

The commissioners appointed by England, probably in consequence of these French overtures to Scotland, met, however, in June 1513, contrary to James' expectation, but "they would not consent to make any redress or restitution till the 15th of October following, believing that by that time they might know the state of the King of England's proceedings in France."

On this being reported to James, he, on the 26th of July 1513, despatched Sir David Lindesay, Lyon King-at-arms, to France with a letter, and with orders to declare to Henry, wherever he found him, that "because of the injuries and wrangis done to him and his subjects by the said King of England, and also because of the present invasion which he made upon his considerate friends, the most christian King of France and Duke of Gueldre, the King of England was therefore requirit to return into his own realme and desist fra the pursuit of the said princes, and to repair and redress the injuries which he and his lieges had sustained, otherwise that the said Lyon Herald must denounce war to him."

Lyon reached Henry VIII. before Terouenne, and "arryving in his army with his cote of arms upon him, he desyrit to speike with the king," into whose presence he was shortly brought by Garter King-at-arms.

Henry received him well, took the letter, and said he would read it.

After he had considered it, he sent for Lyon, and told him that he would give him a verbal answer which he might carry home to the king his master.

Whereupon Lyon said, "Sir, I am the king's natural subject, and he my natural lord, and that he commandis me to saie, I may bauldy saie, with favour; bot the commandments of others I may not nor dare not say to my sovereign lord; bot your letters which your honour may send, I may take with your pleasure; albeit your answer requires doing and no writing, that is, that immediately you should return hame."

Henry replied somewhat hastily, "I will return at my pleasure to your damage, and not at your master's summoning."

Whereupon Lyon declared war, and departed for Flanders, where he hoped to take passage across, but the chronicler adds, "he gat not redie passige, and come nocht in Scotland quhill Floudoun field was strikin and the kinge slain."

Henry meanwhile sent word to the Earl of Surrey that war had been declared to him, and ordered him to send his son, the Lord High Admiral, by sea, capturing the while all that he came across, to Berwick, where they could unite their forces for the invasion of Scotland.

James heard of these preparations in the first days of August, though wondering at his herald not having returned with an answer. He also heard of the Earl of Surrey's presence at Pomfret, and anxious to be first in the field, he allowed Lord Home, Lord Chamberlain and Warden of the Scottish Marches, to invade Northumberland, while he levied an army of between sixty and one hundred thousand men to invade England in earnest.

Lord Home was unsuccessful, though he set fire to twelve villages which he had plundered. Sir William Bulmer, captain of the Palatinate forces, with two hundred archers lying in ambush "amongst the tall broom which then covered the sandy plain of Millfield near Wooler," disposed of three thousand Scotch so effectually, that all the Scotch chronicler has to say is, that "the said Lord Chamberlane eschapeit on the day of ill rode, 13th of August 1513."

On the 22d of August, the herald not having returned, and no war having been openly declared, though the preparations for war on both sides had been tantamount to such a declaration, James IV. at the head of his magnificent army arrived at the village of Coldstream, and crossing the Tweed "with a few cumpany," rode to Twisell, where he encamped, and thence to Ford Castle, the property of Sir William Heron of Ford and Twisell, whose wife the beautiful Agnes is reported in romance to have exercised such a spell over King James.

> "O'er James's heart, the courtiers say,
> Sir Hugh the Heron's wife held sway."

Sir William Heron had been sent some years before a prisoner to Scotland, because of an affray at a Border meeting, when he killed Sir Robert Ker, the Scotch Warden of the Marches. He was kept a prisoner in Fast Castle Tower, in the Mers, on a rock, above the Frith of Forth, and thus it was that his wife was left alone with her step-daughter Margaret, at Ford Castle, which on this occasion was wholly undefended, although some Scotch historians maintain that it was taken by them as if siege had been laid to it.

Margaret, who afterwards married Sir W. Carr, was the last of the Herons and the heiress of their estates.

The charms of Agnes, vaunted as they have been, cannot, however, have exercised much influence on this occasion, for on the 23d, in the afternoon, King James appeared before Norham Castle with all the guns and siege artillery which during a year of peace he had received from France and Flanders for the purpose of being used against England.

Since the siege in 1497, when Garth and Hamerton so distinguished themselves, Norham had been thoroughly repaired, but the items of expenditure on this count, when compared with those which were sanctioned after its capture on the present occasion, clearly prove that the seven "Borthwick" guns and "Mons Meg" were not brought into action against its walls in the first siege.

From the list of expenditure we gather that John Aynsley was in the first instance paid £153 for repairs done between the years 1497 and 1509; and in the year 1510, when King Henry's suspicions of the Scotch intentions were coming to the fore, the expenses for material, ammunition, and wages at Norham amounted to £343, 4s. 6d., while the repairs were completed in 1511 at a cost of £254, 6s. 8d.

The details of this gross total of £750, 12s. 2d., or about £2100 of our present money, show that stones, lime, wood, lead, sand, and coal were the principal items bought, and that the wages paid to the labourers, masons, and carriers formed the greater portion of the expenditure; and the conclusion necessarily drawn is, that the damage actually done to the walls was not of a very substantial nature, and that the firing on the Scotch side was still in its infancy and ill-directed, since a fortnight's bombardment was not productive of any greater damage than the "fall of one tower," for which all these stones dressed in the Tweedmouth quarries were led to Norham.

As soon as "Mons Meg"* was in position in the village of Norham, facing the barbican, her power was tried against it, and in its shock the old castle felt the might of coming ages, and her inability to cope with the murderous weapons which succeeded the days of chivalry.

At the end of two days the barbican was a mass of ruins, and the outer ward was taken by assault.

In the year 1521, Lord Dacre commented on the weakness of this outer ward, and reported that the "outer ward is so feeble that it cannot be kept by reason that the four towers founded for bulwarks is of that lowness, that it is not able to abide a siege;" but of the inner ward he added, "it is so fynished and of that strength that with the help of God and the prayer of St Cuthbert it is impregnable."

Masters of the outer ward, the Scotch could make no impression upon the inner ward, though they damaged the donjeon and the chapel and most of the offices within.

Sir Richard Cholmeley defended himself valiantly, and so did his gunners; but they too were new at the work of artillery, and fired somewhat too rapidly, the result being that by the 25th he ran short of ammunition.

* This gun, cast at Mons in Belgium, and called after Queen Margaret, is now in Edinburgh, and is said to have been used against Norham in 1497.

Seeing this, the Scotch called upon him to capitulate, but Sir Richard declared he would hold out till the 29th even without ammunition, promising at the same time that unless he were relieved by that date he would surrender the castle to King James.

He was thereupon allowed to send a herald to Surrey, who was at Newcastle; but it seems certain that the messenger did not reach the latter in time to allow of his fulfilling his promise to relieve Norham.

The 29th arrived, and anxiously from the old battlements did Sir Richard Cholmeley, a brave soldier himself, scan the horizon in hopes of seeing an army of relief; but at nightfall his hopes went down with the sun, and he marched out a prisoner.

Norham had surrendered; not for long, however, for in less than three weeks she had been reconquered; and it is a curious fact that in her 500 years' history of resistance to Scottish arms she never was, on the three occasions when she was taken, by King David, by Bruce, and by James IV., longer than a month in Scottish hands.

Historians have endeavoured to prove that treachery was at work in the surrender of Norham, and that the belief was strong even at the time is undoubted, as the following will show; but Mr Lamb, whom Dr Raine somewhere calls an "imaginative antiquarian," but whose notes to the "Poem of Flodden" are curious and interesting, founds his belief in treachery on the fact that James IV. was encamped on Ladykirk Bank, that is to say, on the Scotch side, whereas we have positive evidence of his having crossed the Tweed on the 22d of August, to have encamped at Twisell, and to have come before Norham on the 23d.

A traitor, whose name is not given, is supposed to have gone to the king and advised him to descend into the flat ground near the Tweed, now called "Gin Haugh," whence with his cannon he threw down the north-east corner of the castle wall.

This, too, is contrary to fact and to possibility, for from the village the north-east corner could not be hit, and it was the barbican that was first destroyed.

Sir Thomas More, Lord Chancellor of Henry VIII., believed in the treachery, as can be seen in the following epigram, wherein he lays stress on the short-lived pleasure of possessing Norham :—

> " Scote quid oppugnas Norhanam viribus arcem
>   Ante tibi falsa proditione datam ?
> Artibus ergo malis capta fuit arce voluptas
>   Magna tibi forsan, sed brevis illa fuit.
> Teque tuisque malâ, meritâ sed morte peremptis
>   Arx intra est paucos, capta, recepta, dies
> Proditor inque tuo peteret cum præmia regno
>   Mors sceleri est merces reddita digna suo
> Proditor ut pereat, pereat cui proditor hostis
>   Invicta in fatis arx habet ista suis."

There is a field near the castle in which the traitor is supposed to have been hanged, and which is called Hangman's Land; but this, again, refers to the administration of justice by the Norham magistrates.

The following lines may, however, interest the reader:—

> "It was the king's express command
>   To waste with cruel sword and flame:
> A field of blood he made the land
>   Till he to Norham Castle came.
>
> Which soon with siege he did beset,
>   And trenches digged without delay;
> With bombard shot the walls he beat,
>   And to assault it did essay.
>
> The captain great, with courage stout,
>   His fortress fiercely did defend;
> But for a while he lasted out,
>   Till his ordnance did spend.
>
> His powder he did profusely waste,
>   His arrows he hailed out every hour;
> So that he wanted at the last,
>   And at the last had none to pour.
>
> But yet five days he did defend,
>   Though with assaults they him assail'd;
> Though all their strength they did extend,
>   Yet all their power had not prevailed.
>
> Had not there been a traitorous thief,
>   Who came King James's face before,
> That in that hold had got relief
>   The space of thirty years and more.

'Oh king,' quoth he, ' now quit this place,
   And down to yonder vallies draw;
The walls then shall you rend and raze,
   Your batteries will bring them low.'

Which as he said, so did the king,
   And against the walls his ordnance bent;
It was a wretched dismal thing
   To see how soon the walls were rent.

Which made the captain sore afraid,
   Beholding the walls how they reeled;
His weapons all then down he laid,
   And to King James did humbly yield.

So when the Scots the walls had won,
   And rifled every nook and place,
The traitor came to the king anon,
   But for reward met with disgrace.

'Therefore for this thy traitorous trick
   Thou shall be tried in a trice.
Hangman, therefore,' quoth James, 'be quick;
   The groom shall have no better place.'"

Another tradition tells how the king was informed of the weakest side of the castle by a letter fixed to an arrow which was shot over the Tweed into his camp; but this, too, I believe to be a mere legend.

Mr Hutchinson's remarks with regard to the powers of resistance of Norham are of great interest, and tell powerfully how, when the use of artillery came to be a portion of regular warfare, even such strongholds as Norham were unable to cope with the new engines.

"When the outward walls were in repair, and filled with troops; when the oillets and other devices for the garrison's fighting and defence were properly supplied with experienced archers, and the bastions were kept by men of valour, it seems almost incredible that this place could ever be taken by assault. But when there was a regular blockade, and time for mining and raising engines, the defence then consisting of different manœuvres would consequently harass the most powerful garrison; frequent sallies becoming necessary, by which the troops are exposed to the superior numbers of besiegers; incessant watchings and severe duties wear down the greatest fortitude of soul, and scarcity of provisions, with perpetual anxiety, subdue the most vigorous heart. Such are the calamities of a siege, and such were many times experienced at Norham."

Proud of his conquest, James went back to Ford Castle, whither even during the siege of Norham he had several times ridden.

On one occasion, according to Mr Lamb, the king, returning from a visit to Lady Heron, and wishing to cross the Tweed at Norham to his camp at Ladykirk, got into very deep water at the west ford, upon which he made a vow to the Blessed Virgin Mary, that if she would carry him safe to land he would erect and dedicate a church to her upon the banks of the Tweed, a vow which, tradition says, he had not time to fulfil, but which was done for him by heavenly powers, who in a single night built the old Gothic church which still stands, and which is all of stone, even to the roof.

An old inscription on the church, which is almost illegible now, gives, however, the interesting particular, that in the jubilee year 1500, King James erected the chapel to our Lady in gratitude for his miraculous escape from drowning while fording the river Tweed.

As we cannot accept the legend as history, and we cannot believe Sir William Heron, who was twice married, to have had the singular ill luck of finding each of his wives unfaithful to him and enamoured of James, we must come to a conclusion, if more prosaic at least more rational, namely, that in the hurry consequent on the Scotch departure from Norham in 1497, on hearing of the approach of Surrey's army, James IV. got out of his depth, and owed his life to the swimming powers of his horse.

Impatient though his army was to advance,* it is certain that the king unaccountably delayed his march forward; and, according to one writer, it was suspected by many that Surrey, being acquainted with the king's "amorous constitution," privately recommended the Lady of Ford and her daughter to remain in their castle, in order to stay the advances

---

* And why stands Scotland idly now?

. . . . . .
What checks the fiery soul of James?
Why sits that champion of the dames
Inactive?

of the Scotch troops till he could by long marches come up with them.

The weather appears to have been very bad for the time of the year. Bishop Lesley says, "thair wes nevir ane fair day nor scarce ane hour, bot gret cold, wind, and weitt during thair remaining in England, so that onely the principall noble men of the realme nor few cumpanys remaynit with the king,"* an amusing attempt at explaining the battle of Flodden Field by a desertion of the bulk of the Scottish army through the badness of the weather, which is deserving of record.

Meanwhile Surrey had been hurrying to make good his word, "that he should make the King of Scots sorry, or die."

On the evening of the 8th of September, Surrey arrived at Barmoor, where he established his headquarters, the Till river winding slowly and deeply between his army and the Scotch, who were encamped on the ridge of Flodden hill, a low and detached eminence from the ridge of Cheviot.

This position was almost impregnable, but King James had "determined to have his enemies before him on a plain field," and when on the morning of the 9th,

> "The Scots beheld the English host
> Leave Barmoor Wood, their evening post,
> And heedful watch'd them as they crossed
> The Till by Twisel Bridge,"

* Lesley's "History of Scotland," vol. i. p. 93.

he would not allow the English army to be interrupted in their passage across the river, even though this strategical movement on the part of Surrey deprived the Scotch of the Till as a line of defence, and placed the English army between King James and his supplies from Scotland.*

As soon as James considered the moment come for a battle in the open field, contrary to the dying advice of King Bruce, which every Scotch monarch knew by heart, he sent Islay, his herald, to Surrey, with a letter bearing the following words :†

"When it is alleged that we are come to England against our bond and promise, we answer thereto our brother was bound as much to us as we to him;

---

* Lesley tells the story differently to Pitscottie :—"The king wes made to believe be an Inglishman, callit Giles Musgrave, which was his companion and espy, that the same (Surrey's march across the Till) was done for ane pollicie to cause the king and his army to leave the strength, and come down fra the hill callit Flowdoune; and in his doune cumin the Inglis ordinance shot fast and did great scathe, and slew his principal gunners; bot the king's artillery did small scathe, be reason of the hight where they stood, they shot over the English army."—Lesley, vol. i. p. 94.

† According to Stowe, Surrey sent a challenge on the 7th of September from Wooler, dated 5 p.m., and subscribed by Surrey, by his son, by Thomas Lord Dacre, by Lord Clifford, by Henry Lord Scrope, Sir Ralph Scrope, Richard Lord Latimer, William Lord Conyers, Sir John Lumley, Sir Richard Ogle, William Lord Percy, Sir Edward Stanley, Sir William Molineux, Sir Marmaduke Constable, Sir William Gascoyne, Sir William Griffith, Sir George d'Arcy, Sir William Bulmer, and Sir Thomas Strangways, but James did not accept the challenge.

and when we swore last before his embassy in presence of our council, we expressed specially in our oath that we would keep with our brother if our brother kept to us, and not else. We swear our brother broke first with us, and since his doing so we have required divers times him to amend, and lately we warned our brother as he did not us. And this we take for our quarrel, and with God's grace shall defend the same at your fixed time, which we shall abide."

The herald returned, and shortly afterwards a rush was made by the Earls of Huntly and of Home, who commanded the Scotch vanguard, upon the sons of Surrey, who commanded the English vanguard, and the banner of Sir Thomas Howard was beaten down.

"The Scottis vanguard fairlie set on with spears and lang weapons, threw the maist part of the said vanguard of England to the earth, slew mony of thair folkis, and the uthers fled; yit thay quha did escape joinit themselves to thair greit battell."

This "greit battell" was the centre of the English army, commanded by the Earl of Surrey in person, whose rear was under Sir Edward Stanley and Lord Dacre, while on the Scotch side the king commanded the centre, and by him were the Earls of Argyle and Lennox, and his rearguard was under the Earls of Crawford and Montrose.

At four in the afternoon the battle had begun, and by five Lennox and Argyle were slain, and their undisciplined highlanders put to flight, which decided the day.

On seeing their discomfiture, James altogether forgot "his character of monarch and general, and rushed on with the illaudable valour of a common soldier."

The English leaders, cool and collected, preserved their station, from which, while they saw all that was going on, they gave their orders and controlled the actions of their bands.

James, carried away by enthusiasm and excitement, dismounted, and his nobles with him, then rushing forth to the front actually struggled with the mass of English bill-men.*

Bothwell, seeing his king in danger, advanced with his reserves, and valiantly supporting the king's attack, was near capturing the standard of Surrey; but at this critical moment Surrey's son, Admiral Sir Edmund

---

* " They close, in clouds of smoke and dust,
 With sword sway and with lances thrust,
  And such a yell was there
 Of sudden and portentous birth,
 As if men fought upon the earth,
  And fiends in upper air.
 Oh life and death were in the shout,
 Recoil and rally, charge and rout,
  And triumph and despair.
    . . . . .
 Spears shook and faulchions flash'd amain,
 Fell England's arrow flight like rain."
  —*W. Scott,* "*Marmion.*"

Howard, the type of a cool soldier, calling Lord Dacre and his cavalry to his aid, attacked Crawford and Montrose, slew them and routed their forces, while Stanley on the left, wheeling round the eminence, came to his help, and all united their strength against the king and Home, who had been abandoned by Huntly. Though Stanley, having routed the right wing, came upon the rear of the Scotch centre, these arranged in the form of a circle maintained their ground, and disputed the victory till the approach of night.

Home* had been alone successful, and the Scotch centre had not retired when darkness put an end to the fight; but on the morning of the 10th of September, Surrey discovered that the field had been abandoned by the foe, and that he had won a victory of the most decisive character.

Among the dead Lord Dacre found King James IV., lying amidst a heap of his warlike peers and gentlemen, pierced with an arrow and mortally wounded on the head with a bill. The bodies of the Archbishop of St Andrews, James' natural son, four abbots, twelve earls, seventeen lords, four hundred knights, and seventeen thousand others, told how keen the fight had been.

* Besides Lord Home, there were present many members of his clan, and conspicuous among these were the "seven spears of Wedderburn," viz., Sir David Home of Wedderburn and six sons. He and his eldest son George were slain, and the standard which they carried on the occasion still remains in the family of Mr David Milne, who married a Home, heiress of Wedderburn, added her name to his own, and is now resident at Milne Graden.

As soon as the body of the king was found, it was taken to Norham Castle,* and thence to Berwick, where it was identified by two of his subjects who had been made prisoners, Sir William Scott, his chancellor, and Sir John Forman, his sergeant-porter.

The body was pierced by several arrows, the left hand was severed from the arm, and the neck was "laid open to the middle." His last words had been, according to the old poem,—

> "'Fight on, my men . . . . .
> Yet Fortune she may turn the scale;
> And for my wounds be not dismayed,
> Nor ever let your courage fail.'
>
> .   .   .   .   .   .
>
> Thus dying, did he brave appear,
> Till shades of death did close his eyes;
> Till then he did his soldiers cheer,
> And raise their courage to the skies."

The body was embalmed at Berwick, and then conveyed to the monastery of Sheen in Surrey.

Such was the end of a prince who, notwithstanding his frailties, deserves well of his countrymen, for his faults proceeded from a gentle and kind disposition, to which he gave way when the higher duties of the State allowed him to throw off a severer garb.

In the administration of justice, "which he exercised during the time of his reign, he deservit to be

---

* " View not that corpse mistrustfully,
Defaced and mangled though it be;
Nor to yon Border castle high
Look northward with upbraiding eye."

numbreit amangis the best princes that ever regneit abone that nation, . . . and if it had pleased the high will of the Almighty to have lent him longer life, he should have brocht that realme of Scotland to sic flourishing estate as the like in none of his predecessors' days was never yit heard of."

The King of England was before Tournay when the news of the victory reached him, and immediately after a letter from the queen was received, in which she said, "To my thinking this battell hath been to your grace and all your realme greater honour than if ye should wyn all the crown of France;" and added, "For the hastynesse with Rougecroix I could not send your grace the piece of the King of Scots coat which John Clyn now bringeth, in which you see how I can keep my promise, sending you for your banner a king's coat." In a postscript she wrote, "I send your grace herein a bill found in a Scottish man's purse, of such things as the French king sent to the said King of Scots to make war against you."

In the month of October, when Henry VIII. returned to Richmond, he was not unmindful of the services of those who had fought so well at Flodden. To the Earl of Surrey he made a special grant to himself and the heirs of his body, in tail male, of an honourable augmentation of his arms, to bear on the bend thereof in an escutcheon *or* a demi-lion rampant, pierced through the mouth with an arrow within a double tressure *flory* and *counterflory gules*.

Among other English noblemen and knights whose names have been recorded as present at the battle were Richard Lord Nevill, Lord Latimer, Lord Scrope of Upsal, Henry Lord Clifford, Thomas Lord Conyers, Sir Richard Cholmondely of Cheshire, Sir William Percy, Sir Philip Tilney, Sir John Radcliffe, Sir John Mandeville, Sir Christopher Clapham, Sir John Willoughby, Sir William Molyneux, and Sir William Bulmer.

Under the latter were gentlemen of the Palatinate —Grays of Chillingham and Horton, Fosters of Bamborough, Carrs of Wark, Muscamp of Barmoor, Orde of Newbiggin, Selby of Twisell, Collingwood of Etal, Selby of Grindon, Clavering of Scremerstone, Carnaby of Haggerstone, and others.

Thus ended the last real attempt at invasion on the part of Scotland.

Norham had been the last of James IV.'s successes. From its keep, which had not been actually taken but had surrendered for the want of ammunition, the Scotch garrison had seen the distant firing on Flodden field, and almost distinguished the various fortunes of the day.

The Cheshire men who deserted * gave them hope

* Hall, who was present with the king before Tournay, says that "on September 25, 1513, the king received the gauntlet with letters of the Earl of Surrey, and highly praised the earl and the lord admiral his son, and all that were in that valiant enterprise:

as they ran past, until the men of Huntly, who did the same, told another tale, and on the morrow of Flodden no Scotch soldier was seen within the castle. Left to itself for the first time within its history, the moment told of its fallen state.

The age of English chivalry died at Flodden, and the Castle of Chivalry received for a brief moment as a dying token the rash but chivalrous king whom it had helped to find peace in a union with England.

We have come to the end of our historical task. Flodden marks the beginning of an era with which this generation is better acquainted, and with which Norham had nothing left in common.

Built by the hands of a clergy that was doomed to disappear for good or for evil within the next few years, it was meet that the bishop's castle should have run its course before the bishop's downfall.

It had nobly done its duty, had helped Scotland to independence, and England to unity. It had contributed to strengthen the latter in its hours of need, and had thwarted the former's plans in its moments of greatest expectation. It could do no more, and it did no more.

"Sic transeat gloria mundi."

but that the king had a secret letter of the Cheshiremen's flying from Sir Edmund Howard, the earl's son, which caused heartburning, but the king would have no man be dispraised."—Hall's "Chronicle," folio 43, b. 44.

CHAPTER XII.

PATCHING UP.

> " Lost sight of, hidden away out of sight,
> Clasped and clothed in the cloven clay ;
>   Out of the world's way, out of the light,
> Out of the ages of worldly weather,
> Forgotten of all men altogether."—*Swinburne.*

ON the 24th of October 1513, a month after the battle of Flodden, the following letter from Bishop Ruttal of Durham was sent to King Henry VIII.'s almoner Wolsey, who already was making rapid strides in the confidence of the sovereign, and towards his own advancement :—

"As towching the Castell of Norham, thanked be God and Saint Cuthbert it is not so ill as I supposid, for the Dongeon and the Inner ward shall be renewyd shortly ; and if I be not lettyd by the Scots, 1 trust, if all promysses be kept with me, they shall be in better cas than they war by Whitsuntide. I have my smythys working on the iron gates and dorys, my carpenters upon roofs, my masons in divysing for stonys and other necessaries for the re-edifying of the sayd dongeon and Inner-warde, my lime breuners set in wark, and within brief tyme I purpose to send unto the king's grace for commyssions to take warkmen agenst the tyme of year for re-edifying of ye Castell, for I purpose, God willing, to spare no money though I live a poor life till it be fynished."

The bishop dated his letter from Auckland, where, apparently, he was entertaining somewhat sumptuously, for he adds in the same letter:—

"The hospitality of this country agreeth not with the building so greate a wark, for that I spend here wold make many towris. I brought hider with me viii tunne of wyne, and our Lord be thanked, I hafe not two tunne left at this hour, and this is fair utterance in two months."

An entry in the accounts for 1514 bears out the bishop's statement:—

"Paid to William Fraunkelyn, Clerk, my Lord's Treasurer, at different times, for re-edifying and amending the defects of the Castle of Norham, and for the wages of the soldiers there, which Castle was lately thrown down and rased to the ground (prostratum et disruptum ad terram) by the rebellion (*sic*) and cruelty of the Scots, as is indented between Hugh Asshton, clerk, Chancellor of Durham, and William Fraunkelyn, dated 29 April 1514. £1108, 5s. = to £3103, 2s."

A further sum of £113, 18s. 4d. was paid to the same William Fraunklyn towards the end of the year. (£318, 19s. 4d.)

In 1516, a long bill for repairs and provisioning of Norham, amounting to £133, 10s. 7d., was paid to Robert Athe, clerk of the works.

One of the items is "for taking down of the lead at Middleham, and for carrying it to Durham: imprimis to William, Plommar, for 5 days' work, per day 6d., 2s. 6d.; to six labourers for five days, per day a man 4d., 10s.; to my lord's tenants of Cornforht and Medlam for carrying of 44 fodar of lead from Medlam to Durham, 44s.; paid for watching of the lead 3 nights, 12d.; for watching of the vans with lead all a night on the moor, 4d."

This shows that, as Mr Raine observes, the bishop was dismantling one of his castles to repair another.

"John Kowpar, for removing the brewing vessels and copper pans from Stockton Castle to Norham," was paid 20d., and most of the iron and guns and powder appears to have been bought of "Maistar Branleng, a Newcastle merchant," ancestor of the Brandlings of Gosforth Park.

Mr Brandling, who, I believe, now represents this old family, has left Northumberland, and is the husband of Julia Lady Jersey, the daughter of Sir Robert Peel.

In 1517, more lead was carried to Newcastle from Stockton Castle for Norham; and it is interesting to note that the lead was first conveyed to Newcastle to "Maister John Batemanson, the plumber," on which occasion the porters received 10s., and that it was then put on board a ship, at the cost of 33s. 4d. for the freight and carriage to Holy Island.

Between the years 1517 and 1521, a sum of £350 was paid, so that in seven years from the time of the repairs being begun the bishop spent no less than £2000 equal to £5600, besides dismantling two castles.

These numerous accounts, however, had to be audited, and the work performed to be inspected and reported upon.

The Chancellor of Durham, William Franklyn, had intrusted the repairs to Robert Athe (a name still borne in the neighbourhood of Norham), and it was necessary to have the opinion of him who was most interested in the repairs to the castle—namely, of Thomas Dacre, its captain, as to the efficiency of such works.

We have accordingly the following "Answer of Thomas Lord Dacre and Philip Dacre his brodre, deputies to William Dacre, Lord Graistock, to a Bill of Instructions brought by Robert Athe from Mr William Frankleyne, Chancellor of Duresme, the 5th daye of February, the 12th year of the Pontificacion of the said Lord."*

* This report, which is the most important document extant upon Norham, has already twice appeared in print, the first time in the "Archæologia," xvii. 201, and the second time in Dr Raine's "History of North Durham," p. 294; but I need not apologise for its third appearance in print, for no history of the castle could be complete without it, and I have given it therefore

"In the first article my said lord by his writing to his Chancellar of his awn hand bering date at Duresme place besides Westminster upon Saint Swithyn day is desirous to knowe in what suyrtie his castell of Norham standes in and how it shalbe ordred heraftre. In the second article to knowe, how the said castell is furnysshed with vitaill, men and other necessaryes for suyrtie of the same. In the third article that a book might be drawn, how the said castell is and shalbe ordred for ther is so evill reaports maid oppenly to his lordship, that he can not be quiet unto sixche tyme as he knowe the certainte therof. In the iiijth article, that my said lord or this tyme has spoken with the Lord Roos and William Heron for warrauntes for Tymbre, In the vth article, finally to be assertaiyned how every thing is, and shalbe ordred for the savegard and custodie of the said castell to thintent that my lord may be aduertised of the same.

"As vnto thes Articles affor written, as vnto the estate of the Castell the said Lord Dacre saith, that is

as it has been copied for me in the British Museum by the kindness of Mr Maude Thompson, from the Cotton Manuscripts, Caligula, B. viii. f. 249.

The reader will especially note that the height of the long wall between the entrance to the inner ward and the lower gate "next the water" is given as over 14 yards or 42 feet high, which seems to me excessive; and also that much attention was given to stabling, there being actual stables for sixty horses, cow-byres fitted to hold fifty more in time of war, and a room under the chapel turned into a stable for twenty more horses.

to say, not vnknowen to my said lord how it is past and covenaunted by Indenture how many solders, how many warkmen and otheris shuld be kepit in the said castell. In the tyme of peas whiche is kepit in nombre according to the tenour of the same Indenture, And also it is further covenaunted that in the tyme of warr, the said wark shall cease and the Fees and wagies of the same to be Imployed for the sure custodie of the said castell. And now it is more likely to be warr then peas, And if the wark shuld cesse the vttre ward is so feble that it can not be kepit bereason that the four Towres founded for Bulwarkes, is of that lawnes that it is not able to abide a sege and the mantill waull of siche febilnes, without it be countermored whiche can not be done if the wark shuld cesse.

"And as vnto the Inner ward it is so fynysshed and of that strienth, that with the help of God and the prayer of Saint Cuthbert it is vnpringnable.

"The long waull betwix the Inner ward and the nethr yate next the watre is fynysshed redie to the Batalling, And so it mistres no more for a necessitie for it is of hight xiiij yerdes and more besides the avantage of the bank of clene waull in sight.

"Ther is achlers redie hewen, and othr filling stuff redie getten in the quarrey that nightand will fynysshe the said fowr towres being bulwarkes or at the lest will furnysshe thre of them.

"Ther is also one stable maid substantiall of stone and Tymbre in five severall roomes that will serue lx horse, Also ther is a bire made for oxen whiche in the tyme of necessite the oxen being awey will serue 1 horse, Also, ther is vndre the chapell a roum whiche was made affor myn entre, which I have orissed with hek and mangeor for xx horse, And so ther is good stabilling redie at this owr for vixxx horse, besides logies whiche is made for servauntes of none effect.

"And as vnto the vitailling of the said castell, ther is of salt beves in salt Barrelt in thre grete Fates, xliij oxen and kye, besides the common beif dayly spendit and occupied, Also in fisshe iij hogishedes of salt salmon, c salt fisshe besides the store of the house, Also ther is whiche shall alwey be redie vnto grisse Beif com vj fed oxen, and ccccth shepe lieng vndre the castell waull nightly as well for suyrtie of the same as for a necessitie.

"Also ther is corn in the garners, and within the castell in stakes by estimation in whete and rye fourty quarters, In malt whiche is now in making at the castell yate fowr score quarters, whiche cornes is to be kepit for perill and Jepiordie of segeing besides the garners dayly to be occupied.

"And in this case as is affor declared standes the said castell like as Robert Athe has sene every particular of the same which I trust will make reaport accordingly,

"And if it be warr my lordes pleasure must be knowen whedre his lordship will have the wark to go forward or to cesse, for if it contynue, and go forward my said lord must be chargied with the wagies of the same out of his coffres during the tyme of warr, for according to the covenauntes of Indentures the wagies and fees of the warkmen must go and find able men, whiche with thos that is covenaunted to be and remane in tyme of peas shall make the full nombre, of lix for the which I have provided of harnes to be abov ther Jakes of myn awn charge, for the deputie of a complete curase, and for every of the other, ane almane Belett, a Bever and a Sallett, besides the Counte my lordes Tenauntes whiche must com in, as they ar appoynted having mete and drink, with a reward, according to ther service, that is to say.

"The Capitain or his sufficient deputie having with his awn person of his awn charge xiiij persons, that is to say hymself, his servaunt, a chaplain, two cookes a Brewer, besides Childre, a butler, thre hynes being personable men, iij servauntes of the said hynes, a carter, and has but to his wage xx. li., And the constable and a servaunt with hym whiche comyth never here to look at his charge x. li, vj Soldees icheuer at C. s, xxx li, ij porters viij li, iiij wattishmen xvj. li all thes ar kepit and remanes at this day except the constable whiche nothing regardith his charge.

"Also ther shalbe kepit upon the wagies of vj

waullers, vj gonners whiche must have takin out of the thre masons wagies, lx. s. and so every gonner shall have vj ɫɫ x. s. by yere. And the Reversion of the thre masons wagies whiche is xv ɫɫ shall kepe iij soldees, Also ther shalbe kepit upon the c. ɫɫ whiche in the tyme of peas shuld be spendit, of lyme lawborers, wrightes and other artificers xx^{ti} able men, icheuer aftre c. s. a pece by yere. And so the hole nombre of lix besides childre, shalbe kepit according to my covenauntes with the best husbandrie that I can make.

"And if it pleas my Lord that the wark be kepit whiche semes to me must be of verey necessite for my lord's honor and suyrtie of his castell and also for the kinges pleasure and sklandre of yll tonges seing the losse of the said castell before his lordship shalbe chargied with no more out of his coffers but only with the som clvj. ɫɫ that is to say for the masons, wallers and quarriors, lvj. ɫɫ for lyme lawborers and other artificers C. ɫɫ.

"And as for ordinance, it is knowen by Indenture wherof one part remaynyth with Maister Chancellar what remanyth in the said castell, fyrst of strete peces a saker, two fawcons a fawcon of Maister Chancellars, viij small serpentyns going upon iij pare of wheles of metal, a grete slaing of Iron and iij serpentyns wherof one has no chambres as for haggbusshes ther is metely knowe and so we have never one pece nor a serpentyn for the fowr bullwarkes with the two yatehouses in the vttre ward. As for gunpowder ther is metly of it to be doing withal And ther must be certain Brimstone and Saufpeter be provided for to thintent that a gonner may sharpit for I fere me that ther is overmiche cole in it wherby it is somthing flatt, as I perceive it upon my hand when I Burn it.

"And as for arrowes ther is certain of them howbeit bereason of evill keping they want feeres, wherby many of them will do no good vnto suche tyme as a fletcher have them throughe handes, And as for bowes ther is none but only xl^{ti} whiche is of none effect, x of them not able, And therfore ther must be provided for, cth or ccth of good Bowes, for commonstore bowes ar of non effect, And in this case standes my lordes castell, with myn opynyon in every thing Refering the correction therof, adding or mynysshing to my lord and in his absence to maister Chancellar, what informacion soever be made the troughe shalbe knowen at lienth And the service whiche I doo to my lord is not for prouffit but only for his pleasure seing that he is so good lord to me as he is, And also it may appere seing that my son has but xx. li by yere for the whiche he findith xiiij persons, And also his kyn and friendes stand bound by ogligacion in the som of Two Thousand poundes for the sure keping of my lordes castall, And the constable having x li for hymself and his servaunt never loking at his charge for the whiche has his patent made sens the making of myn Indenturs for terme of his life. Howbeit it is covenaunted in the same Indenturs that ther shuld be no Constable but suche as I shuld be content with, Nothwithstanding yf he will do his duytie I shalbe content with hym as wele as with ane oder At my said lordes castell of Norham the vijth daye of February the yere of God a m^l v and xxj$_t^l$ And the xiijth yere of the pontification of the said lord Thomas by the grace of God busshop of Duresme And lord of the Shires of Norham and Eland.

"Thomas Dacre."

Endorsed.—" Tho. 1. Dacre about the fortificacon of Norham Castle. 7° Februarij 1521."

In the above interesting document Lord Dacre points out that "now it is more likely to be war than peace," and surely he had every reason, if such was his opinion, to impress the bishop with the necessity of strengthening Norham, for his Chancellor Frankleyne had a short time before written to say :—

"Please it your good lordship, on Tuesday, the 28th day of August, 1 came to Norham, which is right wele and substantially furnished both with victuall ordynaunce, men and all other necessaries, and so strongly fortified with countermines and murderers that it is now out of all danger, both of gunshot and also of assault. The wall called the long high walle, extending from south-west part of the dongeon to the north-west end of the kitchen, being in length 44 yards and in height 30 foot, is countremined, and the same wall with his contremine is 28 foot thick. The chapel walls 7 foot in thickness, in length 30 foot, and in wideness 18 foot, with a closet over the same, and the battlement of the said closet and long wall all of one height, and so for to go round about from the south-west of the dongeon unto the north-east part of the dongeon."

Nothing, however, came of Dacre's fears in 1521, but in 1523, there being serious apprehensions of a Scotch invasion under the Duke of Albany, Lord Surrey, Norfolk of Flodden's eldest son, surveyed the castles of the Marches, and thus reported to Wolsey, now a cardinal and Bishop of Durham :—

"I have surely viewed the house at Norham all round about, leaving nothing unlooked upon, and have divised divers platforms, ramparts, and mending of broken places with turf and earth, which may be done within six days. The same being performed as Sir William Bulmer has promised, I doubt not, God willing, if the duke come to lay siege, he shall not obtain the same within eight days, by which time I trust to be ready to encounter with him."

In the same letter he, too, dwells on the inefficiency of the outer ward. "It will not be holden one day after the ordnance be laid, wherein there can be no remedy at this time."

Berwick at that time appears also to have lost much of its strength, for in the same report Surrey says :— "For Berwick I fear more than for any of the others, for undoubtedly it is not tenable against a siege royal, having no bulwarks nor fausbrays, nor any defence, but the walls, ramparts and dikes; and as for the castle, if the duke knew how feeble the walls be and and how thin, he would not fail to assay the same, which would not hold out the balles of six cortowles eight hours." Sickness, too, was prevailing in the district at the time, and in the very house in which the Earl lodged in Berwick, "one man died full of God's marks."

In the same report he asks for gunners, of whom he only has "thirty-six, which are too few for Norham and Wark alone," and recommends the dismantling of Dunstanburgh Castle, "that does no good there."

But Surrey knew not the weakness of the Duke of Albany, for although he laid siege to Wark and took it, "peace was keipit all the nixt wintar following betwixt the twa realmes, and thair wes no invaisione one nather syd quhill the moneth of May."

It was on this occasion that the Duke of Albany ventured upon sending a challenge to Surrey, "requiring him apoun his honour to come forduart and he suld meit him at the marche in Scotland and gif him battell," which the earl proudly disdained to accept, informing the duke's herald that he had not come to invade Scotland, but to defend England by commission of his king.

The incident points to the contempt in which Albany was held, but marks also that departure from the old days of chivalry which the introduction of artillery had already completed.

On his way to Barmoor from Alnwick, Surrey stopped at Lowick (indeed he had his headquarters there), which is at right angles between Norham and Wark, and received a message from the prioress of the nunnery at Coldstream, that Albany, having been assured that he was coming, had departed with his army, " complaining of ill health and anxious to be discharged of his command," and dated his letter, " Lowicke, the poure village, in my hall, my kitchen and my bed chamber all in one."

Wolsey, while Bishop of Durham, took a great interest in the Borders, as is evinced by the extensive correspondence which appears during the years of his bishopric; but no great event seems to have marked his passage in that see, except that many of the letters are addressed to him as " Cardinal, Lord Norham," and the appellation is the first and only one of the kind with which we can meet.

The fact is that the history of Scotland during the whole of the sixteenth century, as well as that of Northumberland, is one of private rather than public feuds, of theft, rapine, plunder, and carnage, carried on by those who were to see the law maintained as much as by those who were anxious to set it aside; and the long lists of depredations which are extant only tell of the captains of Norham having for every sheep lost to the Scots taken 100 from them, and for every head of cattle, some 50 in retaliation.

Lord Dacre, the Warden of the Marches, a warrior of distinction, who had materially helped in the success of Flodden, vindicates his loyalty to the throne by enumerating all the harm he has done to the Scotch, "albeit they love me worst of any Englishman living, be reason that I fande the bodye of the King of Scots."

"I assure your lordship for truth that I have and has caused to be brent and destroyed sex times moo townes and howsys within the west and middle Marches of Scotland in the same reason then is doone to us."

Frankleyn, on the other hand, complains that the "Borders of England sore exclaimeth of despoils made unto them by the Scots."

Elsewhere Lord Dacre writes, 29th October 1513: —"On Wednesday at three o'clock afternoon, my brother, Sir Ch. Dacre, assembled diverse of the king's subjects being under my rule, and rode all night into Scotland, and on Thursday in the morning they began upon the middle Marches, and brent the manor place of Trewyn, with the hamlets belonging to them down, continually from the break of day to one o'clock afternoon; and there was took and brought away 400 head of cattle, 300 sheep, certain horses, and very miche household furniture."

The Bishop of Carlisle, writing to Cardinal Wolsey, 1522, says significantly :—" There is more theft, more extortion by English thieves than there is by all the Scots of Scotland.

" In Hexham every market day there is four score or a hundred strong thieves, and the poor men and gentlemen also seeth them which did rob them and their goods, and dare not complain of them by name, nor say one word to them. They take all their cattle and horse, their corn as they carry it to sow, or to the mill to gryne, and at their houses bid them deliver what they will have, or they shall be fired and burnt."

Interesting though these documents undoubtedly are, that tell of these well-planned raids, cruel surprises, and retaliatory acts of violence, so numerous that, as Dr Raine says, "it appears a matter of surprise that the country at large within fifty miles of the Borders on either side should have been inhabited at all, as neither by night or day could a man reckon upon his life or substance for a single hour," still they are foreign to the purpose of this book; and the temptation of describing how not only in times past, but especially at this stage of English history, Northumberland which was so uncultured as to possess only 53 out of 146 county gentlemen who could sign their names to a public document, rose out of a heap of ruins, ignorance, and demi-savage state into its present prosperity, must be reserved to other hands. The subject is inviting; but Norham then was part of Durham, and the bishops of that see were jealous of their prerogatives.

These prerogatives appear to have been of the same kind which the Border robbers claimed, as may be seen by the following letters of Lord Dacre to the Bishop of Durham :—

22d October 1513.—"Ready to make a roodes (inroads) according to order, when moon and weather permit."

23d October 1513.—"I caused four roods to be made in Tevidall—one to the tower of Howpaslot, and there brent, took, and brought away 28 sheep with goods; another rood to Carlanrig, and there brent and wan 4 head of cattle ; and a great rood made by the inhabitants of Tyndale and Reddesdale to the Castle of Ancrum, and burnt the town of the same, and took and brought away 60 prisoners, with much goods, cattle, and insight (household furniture). I cannot attack the Mers—too far off."

That the incursions of the moss-troopers from Scotland, and the rebellion of the Tynedale men, when the family of Charlton especially gave trouble and came into notice,* kept the wardens of the several marches and the Bishop of Durham's lieutenants constantly on the watch, we have abundance of proof; for although unbesieged, Norham continued to be maintained in a state of efficiency, and on two occasions—in 1542 and in 1551—was minutely inspected and reported upon.

In 1542, on the 2d December, Sir Robert Bowes informed the king that "the Castle of Norham, standing nere unto the river of Twede, belonging to the Bishop of Duresme, is in very good state both in reparations and fortifications, well furnished and stuffed with artillery, munitions, and other necessaries requisite to the same."

But in 1551 there came a different report, which is, however, very intelligible, when it be remembered that most of the resources which enabled the Bishop of Durham to maintain his fortresses in a state of efficiency had been forcibly taken from him by a lustful king.

The Marquess of Dorset, Warden-General, having requested Sir Robert Bowes to report to him upon the state of the frontier fortresses, this is what he said about Norham :—

* "As to Tyndale and the E. and M. Marches, I have apprehended three of the most principal headsmen and captains of the same Tyndale—William Charlton of Bellingham, Roger Charlton, his brother, and Thomas Charlton of Caretell, by whom all the inhabitants were governed."

Lord Dacre, Morpeth, 20th May 1524.

"The next hold from Barwick upon Twead is the Castle of Norham, which belongeth to the Bishop of Duresme, who alloweth no mo therein in wages but a captayne, a constable, and two gunners.

"That castle standeth marvellously well for the defence and relief of the country, as well from incourses of enemys in time of war as from thefts and spoils in tyme of peace; for it standeth upon the utter (extreme) frontier, and upon a fray made, or any other warning given by fire beacon or otherwise, the inhabitants of that castle, or a garrison of horsemen lying there, may be in the way of any enemies that shall pass into Scotland between Barwick and Wark, or between Wark and Teversheughe. Also, such as lye in that castle have used in time of need to watch the fordes of Twead between the boundes of Barwick and the mooth of the river Till.

"That castle, for want of continual reparation, is in much decaye, for the first utter walles of the inner ward towards Scotland, endlong the banks of the river of Twead, be much corrupted by occasion that the said wall hath beene covered with leade, but that the rayne water fallinge thereon hath alwaies discended into the walle, and by contynuance hath soe putryfied the lyme and stone of the same that there hath sundry pieces fallen forth of the same. And more is like soe to doe, and as appeareth a small batterye on the north syde from Jeynham, in Scotland, opposite therunto, would bring downe that long walle endlong the halle and kitchen from the newe walle at the stayre or turnpike uppon the north-east corner of the said inner warde, unto the ende of the oven in the kitchen, whiche is a full quarter of the saide inner warde, and leaveth alle the rest thereof open to the sight of Scotland. The said inner warde of that castle is in no place flancked save by a little bulwarke or casamata made in it towarde the utter warde, which flanketh betweene the yates and the doungeon, and maye with hagbuttes heat a great parte within the utter ward, albeit the poynt of that little bulwarke is (by no meanes) warded or flanked.

"The dungeon of the castle hath beene a verye large and strongly bayldid tower of great height, whereof almoste the one halfe hathe beene decayd and fallen longe sithend. It is flanked in no place, save that the said little bulwarke flanketh a great portion thereof towards the utter warde; the gates of the inner warde lye very playne and open, and might wele be more coertly casten and better for defence.

"The utter warde is invyroned towards the est, south, and west with a very old, thynne, and weake wall, save that there be sundry little towers made therein to flank the foote of the said wall, which were not ingenyously devised, for the poynts or grounds of none of the said towers be flanked, but that a man maye come to the poynts thereof without danger of any shote, other than such as is shotte forthe right; and the said walles of the utter warde be both olde and much decayd. There is a place also towards the north side of the said utter warde, at the west end of the chappell, where the wall is soe lowe that a man maye forthe of Scotland, upon the bank head towards the Lady Church, view and see any man that stirreth within the said utter warde, specially in passage from the upper gate into the inner warde, which would be amended with no great charge.

"Fynally, that castle, standing in soe meete a place for the defence of the frontier and country thereabouts, were convenient (as we thinke) to be in the kinges ma^{tyes} handes, and soe would it be better repayred and maynteyned then it is.

"And if it were the kinges ma^{ties} castle, first the wall of the utter warde being amended, as it might be with no great charge, and shedds or toofalls made toward the inner side of the same from the south-east corner thereof to the north-west part wher the gate hath gone of old tyme towardes the towne, the same tyme of warre, when enymies did invade; and therein also might be their soldiers lodged and stabling for their horses, one hundreth and mo horsemen in tyme of warr; those shedds and toofalls being made bylowe for stables, and a lodging abone for souldiers. The iron gate of the utter warde lie hong very unwisly uppon the utter side, for the enemyes may come and pike the crukes of them forth of the wall, whan they might hang better to purpose ynnermor in that gatehouse in a payre of wood gates without them to cover them.

"Also the olde gates, towardes the towne at the north-west corner of the saide utter warde were best, as we think, to be mowved upp and a privy postern couertly conveyed that waye, which might serve either for assayly to yssue forth of the castle, towards the rescues of the towne for a suddayne, or ells if the inhabitants of the towne being overlayed with enemies, retyred to the castle, they might most readily that way be received in. And for the most sure fortifying the inner warde, myne opynion were to have that uppon the north-east corner of the dungeon, to be massively rampired with earth, both to the hall and kitchen and other houses in that part. And the hall to be made in that part of the dungeon that is decayed, which might be with no great charges (in respect of a king's worke) made to or three howses high above the vault that nowe standeth. And the nethermost of the houses, to be the hall, buttery or pantry. And yet the last end thereof to be fower and twentieth foote, rampired within the utter wall and the other two heightes above that would serve for lodgings for the captayne and his howshold. And the dungeon being nowe overhighe, might be taken downe one story, leaving only the turnpike thereof for a watch howse. And the stone taken of the dungeon head, would all moste serve to make upp the walles of the decayed parte of the saide dungeon soe thick as they be standing inward towarde the saide inner warde. And the lead and tymber of the hall and kitchen would almost serve for the roufes and floures of the said parte of the dungeon, which shoulde be reedifyed, and then should all the saide inner warde be strongly rampired round about. Also the gates at the entrye of the inner warde would be (as I think) where the gates nowe enter towards the west, rampired for a cowered gate. And the waye more couertly conveyed to passe by the rampire at the east ende of the chappell, and soe to come forward to the north, and the wall of the gatehouse unto the entry that now is, and soe eastward in at the iron gates that be nowe. I thinke also if it were thought convenient, there might be bulwarks or casamats made without the wall to flank the north and east side of the said inner warde, which I refer to more ingenious men such feates than I am."

Contrasting these two reports, the rapid strides of events must explain their singular discrepancy, for while the report of 1542 was written when the Bishop of Durham was still in possession of all the revenues of his bishopric, Sir Robert Bowes was only acting as the lieutenant of a bishop, and had no great desire to find fault with a castle which, as he says, should be " in the king's majesty's hands;" but ten years later when the suppression of the small monasteries had taken place, when the privileges of the Palatinate had been withdrawn, and the means of the bishopric to strengthen Norham had been curtailed, the same Sir Robert finds everything wrong, and conceiving the possibility of the crown taking the castle in its own hands, points how the crown can spend its money.

But the two reports are even more instructive, showing as they do the progress which a soldier like Sir Robert Bowes had made in military matters between the dates of each.

When the first report was written, belief in the power of the English archers had not altogether vanished, and hence the confidence in the old walls of defence had not altogether disappeared; but by 1551 such confidence had gone for ever, and the possible improvements in the art of gunnery had to be considered.

With this view all about the old castle was necessarily wrong, and instead of walls, "ramparts of earth" were to be the new order of defence.

But even ramparts require labour, and labourers require to be paid; and although W. Bennet, master of the king's ordnance at Berwick, was paid £7, 10s. for 1¼ ton of Spanish iron to be used at Norham, and 53s. 4d. were paid to Cuthbert Fletcher for endeavouring to secure workmen at Berwick, "ridynge sundry times from Northam to Berwick to gytt license for warkemen to come from Berwick to worke at Northam," not much appears to have been done for the old fortress, for in a letter dated 30th September 1557 from one Richard Norton to the Earl of Shrewsbury, the following passage occurs:—

"Since I am informed that the Scots will not fail to besiege Norham as they intend, wherefore I thought meet for mine own discharge to declare the estate of that house. There is but in powder two barrels; which last is too little as good gunners say. There is but one gunner that my Lord of Durham sent yesterday, and one that was there before who has discharged himself because he saw no help, and is offered better entertainment, and two gunners are too few besides him. If a siege comes there lacks weapons, bills and pikes with baskets; there are none neither for the walls nor for to carry to fill up breaches. No balls nor trunks to amuse the enemy with, nor as yet know I not what companie shall be assigned to remain with me in the house and towne. I shall not fail my part, God willing, otherwise it is but a casting away of the house and of them that are in it."

In 1559 the temporalities of the shires of Norham and Island were for ever alienated from the See of Durham, because Bishop Tunstall refused to take the oath of supremacy to the "maiden queen."

The act recited that "upon the voidance or vacation

of any archbishopric or bishopric, the queen was empowered to take into her hands as much of the honours, castles, &c., belonging to the same as shall amount to the clear yearly value of all parsonages appropriate and yearly tenths belonging to the crown in the same, and was enabled to discharge the succeeding bishop from the payment of such tenths accordingly."

The value of the See of Durham in the queen's books, which had been £2821, 1s. 5d., was put down at £1821, 1s. 5d., and Norham and Island constituting a part of the reserved territory, the sum of £1000 yearly was paid to the crown as rental of such reserved property.

It was time that the castle should fall into ruins, when the crown wanted its possession merely to farm it out at interest.

It had shown signs of decay. Queen Elizabeth hastened its destruction.

CHAPTER XIII.

DECAY.

> "Though thou art fall'n, while we are free,
> Thou shalt not taste of death;
> The generous blood that flow'd from thee,
> Disdain'd to sink beneath,
> Within our veins its currents be
> Thy spirit on our breath."—*Byron*.

ALREADY, in 1524, Lord Dacre, writing to Cardinal Wolsey, said, "There is little left upon the frontiers except old houses, whereof the thak (thatch) and coverings are taken away, so that they cannot be brent," and we have seen to what poor condition the castle had been reduced after the siege.

Notwithstanding this, Roger Lassells, writing to the "Cardinal Norham," 8th September 1828, from Norham Castle, said :—

"Apon Saturday the v day of September, the Earl of Anguishe, the Abbot of Holyrowdhous, come to Tweedside, and callyd over upon me and descried me that I would come and speek with thaym; and so I did, and the said earl askyd me if that I knew the king's gracious pleasure and my lord cardinal's, as my lord cardinal dyd promise his servant to send to your lordship, and I shewed him that I supposed verily that your lordship had no farther knowledge since your servaunt come home. Whereof he had great marvel, desiring me that he might have a chambre for his daughter which he had with the Queen of Scots and the young Earl of Huntly, and the wife of Archibald Douglas to wait upon them, and another chamber for himself, the Abbot of Holyroodhowse, George Douglas and Archibald Douglas, if he be of necessity driven thereunto, and those that be his partakers, he desireth that they may be in the town of Norham two or three days unto such time as the king return homeward and scail his host.

"And I have promised him that if the king come with his great hoste, I shall suffer him to be in Norham Castle and in the town unto such time as I shall know farther of your lordship's pleasure."

No words could better describe the subservient spirit which was gaining under the strong rule of Wolsey, and the cautious temper of his lieutenants.

The Angus here referred to was Archibald, seventh Earl of Angus, who was married three times.

His first wife, daughter to Patrick Hepburn, died in childbirth "within the year of her marriage as they say, immediately after the field of Flodden," and his second wife was Queen Margaret, the widow of James IV., killed at Flodden, and daughter of Henry VII.

The daughter alluded to in the despatch of Lassells is the Lady Margaret Douglas, the issue of this second marriage, who married the Earl of Lennox, and was the mother of Henry Darnley, who married Mary Queen of Scots, and by her had a son, James VI. of Scotland "and first of Great Britain."

Here, then, was the grandmother of England and Scotland's first joint sovereign knocking for admission at the gates of Norham Castle.

In 1542 some suspicion of treachery was put forth, so as to facilitate the gradual absorption of ecclesiastical lands in the hands of the crown.

The Duke of Norfolk received a letter from the Archbishop of Canterbury, dated 20th September, purporting thus: "Whereas the king's highness is informed that a certain treason concerning the delivery of Norham Castle to the Scots in such sort as your lordship may perceive by a schedule herein enclosed (which has not yet been found), you will cause the place in secret wise to be serched, and try whether there be any parson in the house mete to be suspected, and take order as convenient."

The suspicion was probably aroused by the fact of France sending more guns and ammunition to Scotland, of which in England they had had easy notice, for we find that "on the penult day of October, the King of France send in Scotland 1000 crowns and 50 piece of artillery," although be it remarked negotiations for peace were going on at the time. If treachery was suspected in 1542, indifference was the watchword in the castle in 1557, when Lord Westmoreland writing, 19th August, to the Earl of Shrewsbury upon a successful raid upon his troops before Norham, says, "It is said the most part of our men that had the last overthrow were taken before the gates of Norham and between the bridge and the iron gates, as it was reported to my Lord of Northumberland and my Lord Wharton at supper the same night. There was not past four men within the castell who shot not so much as one hasquebush to relieve any man.

"The old custom hath been that when a fray came, all the country brought their goods and chattels into the hollow ditches under the walls, where they were as safe as within the castel, nor it was never seen before that any Scot durst come near the castell, but now they went into the hollow ditches where they took 30 score sheep, with a great number of cattle, and none to resist them, nor yet so much as one man to cast down a stone over the walls at them.

"Tempora mutantur et nos mutamur in illis."

Men, times, customs, buildings, all were changing, and the above letter, sad as it reads, remains a standing proof how mighty had been the fabric which on its decay could bring forth such sentiments.

This was the year when the Carrs of Ford, aided by the Collingwoods, disputed with the Herons of Chipchase their claims to the castle of Ford, and the whole county took part in the quarrel, the result being that justices of the peace dared not hold their usual session at Morpeth, and that these Northumbrian Montagues and Capulets, while destroying each other, united against the king's lieutenant of the Marches, Lord Wharton.

"We think this hundred years forepassed never happed there so perilous a seed of malice, full dissension and hatred to be sown in this country as is presentlye in planting, and like to take root if not hastily met withall and prevented."

At last the decay of the bishop's power was complete. On the 13th October, Lord Westmoreland, writing to Lord Shrewsbury, says:—

"The bishoprick men doth covet to come home, there pass not 400 of them. Your lordship told me there was a hundred horsemen of the bishopric, but I believe it will fall out there is no horsemen here but mine, except it be Robert Tempest. I have seen the bishopric service at such a time with a thousand men, but it will be so no more."

It was "so no more," for in less than two years from the date of this letter Norham had become a portion of crown property, which might be sold or given at the will of the sovereign.

But it was not the habit of the queen who now reigned to allow matters to be half done; and before disposing of her newly acquired property, she wished to know its strength and its value.

In "the order taken the second year of the queen (20th August, 3 Elizabeth, 1561) for her fortifying the Borders," we have a long list of commissioners, among whom were Sir Henry Percy, knight, Captain of Her Majesty's castles of Tynemouth and Norham; Sir George Bowes; Thomas Carns, serjeant-at-law; and Valentine Brown, Esq., treasurer of Berwick.

These commissioners appointed gentlemen of the county—"Sir John Witherington, knight; Thomas Foster, George Heron, Nicholas Ridley, Alban Featherstonhaugh, Cuthbert Carnaby, Robert Clavering of Callalie, Robert Mydleton of Bellrowe, James Ogle, Esquires; Thomas Collingwood, John Selby the elder, John Carre of Ford, Ralph Collingwood of Tythington, gentlemen—to view and survey the execution of the premises, for the queen wishes to put in force a statute, 2 and 3 of Philip and Mary, for the inclosures of grounds within twenty miles of the Borders of Scotland, so as to protect them against murders and robberies."

This commission recommended that "little crofts or closes be enclosed of the lands next adjoining every town, village, or hamlet, so as to strengthen the town, village, or hamlet.

"2. That each field should be surrounded by a hedge and a ditch.

"3. All commons and wastes within twenty miles to be ditched round.

"4. Several castells, towers, houses, barmekins, tounes, and villages having been found in great ruin by reason of wars, a certain undetermined sum shall be set aside yearly for their repair by their owners, a sixth of the income, however, having to be expended on repairs in the event of the castle or house, &c., having fallen into decay by reason of the negligence of its possessor."

As to Norham it was remarked that, "entrance being easy by the Tweed between Berwick and Cheviot, the lords, owners, farmers, &c., of towns, &c., within four miles of Tweed, shall at their common costs, by order of the Captain of Norham, make near the fords ditches of 6 foot deep and 8 foot broad before All Saints next."

Then follows a list of the names of those lords, freeholders, tenants, and inhabitants that "have consented and agreed to the above articles"—

Lords Northumberland, Dacre, Ewryc, and Ogle, all of whom could sign their names; Sir John Dallyrell, knight, who also signed.

Three Ogles who could write, and six who put a cross in token of their inability to sign their names.

Four Fosters signed, one put a cross.

Two Grays signed.

Six Herons, of whom four could not sign.

One Clavering, who signed.

Two out of three Ridleys could write.

Two out of four Collingwoods could write.

Only one out of twelve Fenwicks could sign his name.

Two out of three Selbys signed.

Not one of the five Erringtons could write.

Two out of the four Carnabys signed.

And as to John Clennell, Edmond Crostor, John Burrell, Oswald Midford, Francis Armer, a X marks their inability to sign their names.

Following upon this survey came a statement of the charges of the East Marches, and of the pay of the garrison of the several fortresses on the Border.

At Norham it was stated that there was or should be a captain of horsemen, whose wages were 6s. 8d. a day; a lieutenant, at 3s. 11d. a day; 24 horsemen, at 10d. each man; an ensign-bearer, at 20d.; a trumpet, at 16d.; a porter, at 10d.; an under-porter, at 6d.; a master gunner, at 12d.; a quartermaster gunner, at 8d.; 16 gunners, at 6d.; one chaplain, at 16d.; and a surgeon, at 16d.—bringing up the total cost of keeping the castle properly manned to £11, 8s. 8d. a day.

The old usages also had been superseded, and extended powers had been given to the captains of Norham, holding as they did that property for the benefit of the crown.

"This captain hath in rule all Norhamshire, and the rents growing to the queen in the right of the bishopric within the same, whereby he hath all the farmers and tenants at commandment for service, which farmers and tenants he must see sorted into horsemen and footmen, furnished with horse, armour, and weapon meet for the wars, to attend the queen's service at all times when he shall call ; in the which shire he hath both pasture and water sufficient, fish and flesh. What estate he hath therein I know not, but wish that neither he nor any man else had any estate in any ground of the queen's majesty belonging to any castell longer than he serveth in that place."

The result of this enactment was a clear inducement to men of enterprise to become possessors of a place which, by the privileges attached to it, was a lucrative post as well as one of honour.

In the reign of Elizabeth, however—a sovereign of whom this realm may justly be proud, albeit a portion of her subjects felt her power in the direst fashion, " At home she threatened particular persons, and they felt her anger ; abroad she threatened kingdoms, and they felt her power "*—this was not possible, and favour alone with Her Majesty was a passport to advancement.

Lord Hunsdon, Governor of Berwick, had a son, Robert Cary, born in 1560, of pleasing manners and good appearance, who, when seventeen years of age,

* Preface to the " Memoirs of Robert Cary, Earl of Monmouth." London, 1759.

became aide-de-camp to Lord Essex, then commander of the English forces in France.

On the disgrace of this nobleman young Cary hurried to the queen in London, and so touched the willing feelings of Elizabeth that he obtained the reinstatement of his patron, who, "as soon as he saw him, drew his rapier, and running up to him laid it on his shoulder and knighted him."

Shortly after his return to England Sir Robert Cary married the heiress of Witherington, and was made Governor of the East Marches in the absence of his father, who could not return to Berwick before he had "borrowyde £1000 of a merchant, of which the interest comes not to £100" (8th June 1584), "for the intertaynment of Barwyke and the wardenry," and on his death became absolute warden in his place, with the grant of Norham, 1593.

On becoming possessed of the castle an inventory was made for him of the goods therein, and which had previously been placed in the charge of his brother William, a captain in the army, then deceased.

This inventory, made on the 25th of March by Captain Carvile and Hector Widdrington, gives the following items :—

IN THE HALL.

Two armours of proof,	£2 15 0
Two cuirasses (curates),	1 10 0
A plackett,	0 4 0
A black target of proof,	0 10 0.

	£	s	d
Ten muskets and a bastard musket,	10	0	0
Four callyvers,	1	0	0
A pair of mail sleeves,	0	10	0
A case of pistols,	0	10	0
Nine black moryons,	0	9	0
A graven moryon,	0	6	8
A gilt rapier and dagger,	0	10	0
A Scottish sword,	0	6	0
A rapier varnished black,	0	6	8
A drum and a case of fifes,	2	0	0
A steel cap,	0	2	0
A presse,	0	8	0
A jack and sleeves of plate,	0	13	4
A two-handed sword,	0	10	0
	£22	10	8

In the Stable.

	£	s	d
Two cotch horses,	£8	0	0
One cotche,	8	0	0
Plate, 102 ounces,	25	10	0
	£64	0	8

On the 24th March 1603 Queen Elizabeth died, and that very morning Cary, to use his own words, "took horse between nine and ten o'clock and rode to Doncaster. On the Friday night I arrived at my own house of Witherington, and gave order the next morning the King of Scotland should be proclaimed King of England at Morpeth and at Alnwick. On the Saturday I took horse for Edinburgh, and came to Norham about twelve at noon, so that I might well have been with the king at supper-time, but I got a great fall, and my horse with one of his heels gave me a great blow on the head, that made me shed much blood. It made me so weak that I was forced to ride a soft pace after, so that the king was nearly gone to bed by the time that I knocked at the gate of Holyrood House.* I was quickly let in, and carried up to the king's chamber. I kneeled by him, and saluted him by his title of England, Scotland, France, and Ireland. He gave me his hand to kiss, and bade me welcome. After he had long discoursed of the manner of the queen's sickness and of her death, he asked what letters I had from the council. I told him none; and acquainted him how narrowly I escaped from them. And yet I had brought him a blue ring from a fair lady, that I hoped would give him assurance of the truth that I had reported.† He took it, and looked upon it and said, 'It is enough; I know by this you are a true messenger.' Then he committed me to the charge of my Lord Hume, and

* Not bad riding, two days from London only!

† "King James kept a constant and private correspondence with several persons of the English court during many years before Queen Elizabeth died. Among them was Lady Scroop, sister of Sir Robert Cary, to whom His Majesty sent by Sir James Fullarton a sapphire ring, with positive orders to return it to him by a special messenger as soon as the queen was actually expired. Lady Scroop had no opportunity of delivering it to her brother Sir Robert Cary whilst he was in the palace of Richmond; but waiting at a window till she saw him on the outside of the gate, she threw it out to him, and he well knew to what purpose he received it."—Preface to the "Memoirs of the Earl of Monmouth."

gave streight command that I should want nothing. He sent for his cherurgions to attend me, and when I kissed his hand at my departure he said to me these gracious words, 'I know you have lost a near kinswoman and a loving mistress; but take here my hand, I will be as good a master to you, and will requite this service with honour and reward.'"

The next day he was sworn a gentleman of the king's bed-chamber; and continues Cary:—

"Now I was to begin a new world. My office of the wardenry ceased and I lost the pay of forty horse, which were not so little as a thousand pounds per annum. I relied on God and the king. The one never left me, the other, shortly after his coming to London, deceived my expectation."

To set himself right, he proceeded to sell Norham Castle.

"Having nothing but Norham to live on, my good Lord of Hume, Earl of Dunbar, begged the keeping of it over my head, and I did see it was folly to strive, and therefore thought on the next best course to do myself good. Dunbar thirsted after nothing more than to get of me the possession of Norham. My Lord Cecil was umpire between us; he offered five thousand pounds; I held it at seven thousand; six thousand pounds was agreed upon, which was truly paid, and did me more good than if I had kept

Norham; and I sold him as much goods therein as I received eight hundred pounds for."

Our task is done; and without laying too great a significance upon the fact, it may seem strange to the reader, as it does to us, that while Scotland's independence had been recognised before the gates of Norham, while a broil from the garrison of Norham had occasioned that historical marriage which made it possible for James VI. of Scotland to become James I. of England, it was the owner and captain of Norham Castle who was the first to salute James VI. as "King of England, Scotland, France, and Ireland."

It is gratifying to find that when the old castle was at last offered for sale, it was bought by the descendant* of that first Earl of Dunbar whose tomb rested already in the church of Norham; and it is significant of how small things have their interest, that for the 600 years during which Norham Castle

* He was the third son of Alexander Hume of Manderston, a favourite of James VI., who appointed him gentleman of the bedchamber in 1585, master of the wardrobe in 1590, and High Treasurer of Scotland in 1601.

He was made Chancellor of the Exchequer in 1603, and created Baron Hume of Berwick in 1604, Earl of Dunbar in 1609, and a Knight of the Garter.

He died in 1611, poisoned by "some tablets of sugar given him for expelling the cold by Secretary Cecil," and left two daughters, coheiresses—Anne, married to Sir James Hume of Cowdenknows, and Elizabeth, to Theophilus, Earl of Suffolk.

had stood the price fixed for its purchase was £6000.

The lands which the crown had appropriated, and which went with the castle, included the estates of Horncliffe, Loanend, and Longridge.

These estates have since passed through many hands—Ordes, Fenwicks, and Blakes—but the ruins have not fared the better for it.*

"How came this waste and wilderness of stones?"

Little remains to tell of past opulence or past grandeur, but what there is still marks the pride of power, and with the poet we yet will say—

"To weep would do thy glory wrong,
Thou shalt not be deplored."

* "Others, as Bamborough, Norham, Wark, &c., and innumerable more, are sunk in their own ruins by the mere length of time."—"Travels of Daniel de Foe," reprinted by Richardson, 1845.

FINIS.

www.ingramcontent.com/pod-product-compliance
Lightning Source LLC
Chambersburg PA
CBHW031336230426
43670CB00006B/343